# THE CABLE KNITTER'S GUIDE

## 50 PATTERNS, 25 PROJECTS, COUNTLESS TIPS AND IDEAS

DENISE SAMSON

TRAFALGAR SQUARE
North Pomfret, Vermont

In memory of my sister, Mona.

This book is dedicated to Anne and Toril—
for their enduring and inspiring friendship.

First published in the United States of America
in 2016 by
Trafalgar Square Books
North Pomfret, Vermont 05053

Originally published in Norwegian as *Hekta på fletter: Et oppslagsverk i flettestrikk.*

Copyright © 2015 Cappelen Damm AS
English translation © 2016 Trafalgar Square Books

ISBN: 978-1-57076-792-0

Library of Congress Control Number: 2016955566

Interior designer: Laila S. Gundersen
Photography: Guri Pfeifer Foto
Patterns and diagrams: Denise Samson
Translator: Carol Huebscher Rhoades

**Printed in China**
10 9 8 7 6 5 4 3 2 1

# CONTENTS

# PREFACE

Every time I see someone knitting cables, I get curious and have to look and see what the pattern is. It's just so fascinating to see stitches that twist over and under each other; there are so many possibilities for making pretty cable patterns, and the results are always so appealing. It doesn't take much cabling on a sweater or a pillow to immediately make it more exciting. And cabling is so much fun! It's a little like knitting stripes in different colors—I'm always so eager to find out how the next cable crossing will look.

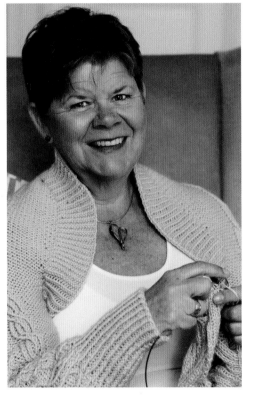

I don't know how many times I've heard friends say, "I'll never be able to knit cables, they look so difficult." But they're not so hard once you've learned how to do them. For simple cables, you don't even need a cable needle to work them.

For the most part, cable knitting involves one or several stitches that change places on the knitting needle, but there are exceptions. Some patterns are constructed so that they only look like cables and you don't need an extra needle. For other patterns, you slip some stitches to a cable needle and wrap the yarn around the stitches, which creates a wonderful effect. I'll show you how you can knit reversible cables, too, which are the best choice for projects like throws where both sides are going to be visible.

Knitting with a cable needle isn't very difficult once you get the hang of it, and you can make an unbelievable number of lovely designs. You just need a little patience at the beginning. Once you're comfortable, you'll even discover a little challenge waiting—three of the patterns are worked using two cable needles.

In the first part of the book, I describe many different cable techniques; in the second, I discuss how you can use and combine the cable patterns in various designs. You'll find everything from easy mug cozies and potholders to larger pieces like throws and cardigans. Once you've learned the symbols for the various cables that are shown on the charts, you'll soon be an expert at cable knitting. Each of the cabling techniques included has its own QR code; if you have a smart phone or tablet, you just have to download a QR app and scan the code to see a video demonstration. (If you don't have a smartphone, never fear—the URL for my YouTube channel where all the videos are posted is also included.)

And, best of all? On page 6, you'll find the recipe for an amazingly good cable-braided bread.

Denise Samson

# A LITTLE HISTORY

Cable patterns originated in the Aran Islands, which lie off the west coast of Ireland—this is why a traditional sweater with multiple cables is often called an Aran sweater. These traditional sweaters are most often knitted with unbleached 100% wool yarn. Earlier in history, they were worn by fishermen and farmers. The sweaters were knitted with unprocessed wool that retains its natural oil, lanolin, which is water-resistant and provides good protection against rain, wind, and cold. That kind of sweater could absorb 30% of its weight in water before it felt damp against the body.

Originally, women were primarily knitting these sweaters just for family members; but in 1892, local knitters in the islands began to sell their work through, among other outlets, the Congested District's Board for Ireland—an organization working against poverty and hardship. At the time, the sale of Aran sweaters was a large part of the islands' income, and local knitters and designers had the opportunity to produce new pattern combinations.

In the old days, none of the pattern combinations were made by chance—quite the opposite. Traditional sweaters are connected to particular clans and their identity. By examining a pattern combination, you could tell which clan the person was from; this information was very useful when identifying bodies washed onto shore after a shipwreck. The symbols in the pattern motifs were said to have special meaning. The traditional cable that is knitted over four or more stitches symbolized rope and represented a wish for good fishing out at sea. A diamond motif represented a patch of ground on the islands; a diamond filled with seed stitch symbolized kelp, which was used in agriculture to ensure good crops. Therefore, the diamond symbolized a wish for riches and success. The honeycomb pattern was also regarded as a symbol of wealth.

At the Aran Sweater Market on the Aran Islands, you can see the public register of these historic patterns.

The first commercially-available knitting patterns with Aran motifs were published in 1940 by Patons and Baldwins in England. Vogue Magazine published some articles about the garments in 1950 and exports from the west coast of Ireland to the USA began in the 1950s. This gave work to women all over Ireland. Even now, the popularity of Aran sweaters continues to grow. However, the lack of proficient knitters and the economic gain brought by mass-produced, machine-knit garments have meant that hand-knitted garments are almost impossible to find on the islands now. Hand-knitted garments are quite valuable and rare. A finished Aran sweater contains about 100,000 precisely worked stitches and can take up to 60 days to make because of the complexity of the patterns.

Today we find cable knitting on many other kinds of garments and accessories, but Aran sweaters will always be a symbol of timeless beauty, synonymous with pride in Irish cultural heritage.

## About Cable Knitting

Most cable patterns, from the easiest to the most complicated, are worked using the same technique—one or more stitches change places in the fabric. In order to accomplish this, you can use a cable needle or a cable hook but you can even rearrange the stitches on the needle by hand if you are only crossing one or two stitches. I'll come back to this later. You can cross stitches both to the right and to the left. So that the cable pattern will stand out, you can work purl stitches, garter stitch, or seed stitch on each side of the cable. Some patterns are worked such that you transfer a certain number of stitches from the left needle to a cable needle, take the yarn and wrap it around the stitches on the cable needle, and then return the stitches to the left needle. No stitches have changed places but the effect and pattern are especially pretty.

Once you understand the technique of knitting cables, you can knit even the most complicated patterns—and I can promise you that you will earn much praise for your finished pieces.

**One general tip that is important to remember is that, when the cable moves to the right, hold the cable needle behind the work and, when it moves to the left, hold the cable needle in front of the work.**

# ZOPF

## (Swiss braided loaf)

I grew up in a baking family. My great-grandfather established the bakery W. B. Samson AS in 1894 on Eger Square in Oslo. Later on, it moved to Frogner, where it's still going in full production. I really should have been a pastry chef like my father, but since I lacked skills in drawing—which are important for a baker—it was office administration that became my career until 2010. Then there were other balls—in the full meaning of the word. The company Andre Boller became a reality and, since that time, I have translated more than 25 books about crochet and knitting. At the same time, I began sending knitting and crochet designs to the weekly magazines.

Still, I haven't stopped baking because of that. I often visit a dear friend in Switzerland and Zopf is a typical Swiss treat on the breakfast table on Sunday mornings. The bread had originated before 1256 when the first Swiss bakery was established. Going into a Swiss bakery is as satisfying as going into a yarn store, especially when one has grown up in a family where bread and cakes have always been in focus. Swiss baked goods are not just good; they are pretty also.

Some think that Zopf has its origins at the time when women cut off their hair braids and buried them with their husbands who had died. As time went on, they buried a braided loaf instead of their hair. This tradition has been known in Switzerland since the middle of the 1500s.

## ZOPF

**Ingredients (makes 2 loaves)**
**6⅓ cups (900 g) all-purpose flour**
**7 oz or 1¾ sticks (200 g) unsalted butter**
**1 egg + 1 egg for brushing on**
**2 cups (½ liter) milk**
**1¾ oz (50 g) fresh yeast or 2 teaspoons (15 g)**
**    dried active yeast**
**½ teaspoon sugar**
**3-4 teaspoons salt**

Sift the flour into a bowl and make a well in the center. Dissolve the yeast in the cold milk and add the sugar. Separate the egg yolk and white. Carefully blend the egg white into the milk and yeast mixture. Stir in the salt. Melt the butter. Pour the butter and egg yolk into the flour. Pour in the yeast and milk mixture. Mix and then knead the dough until smooth. Cover the dough with a kitchen towel and leave to rise in a warm place for 1 hour.

Divide the dough into four equal pieces and roll each piece into a "sausage," with the center thicker than the narrower "tails."

*Here comes the hard part.*

You'll need two lengths for each Zopf loaf. Lay the first length on the table horizontally and then place the other piece vertically on top of it, at the center (the pieces make a cross). Fold from the center of the lengths so that all four ends point diagonally downwards. Take each end of the bottom length and cross them over each other. Do the same with the ends of the top. Continue alternating crossing each length until the braid is complete. Press the ends together well. The braid should be thick at the top and narrower at the bottom. If you have trouble making the braid, you can search for Zopf on YouTube.com. You'll find several good videos about how to form the braids for a real Swiss Zopf.

Alternatively, you can braid the loaf using three lengths, the way you might braid hair; or you can twist the lengths together from the top like a rope, fold the lengths in two, and then twist once more.

Twist the braid the same way for the second loaf. Don't worry if the two loaves are not identical. They will taste equally good!

Transfer the loaves to a baking sheet lined with baking parchment.

Brush both loaves with egg wash (whisk the second egg with a small amount of water). Bake the loaves in a 400-430ºF / 200-220ºC oven for about 40 minutes. Increase the heat towards the end of the baking time to ensure that the tops are a fine brown color.

*Bon appetit!*

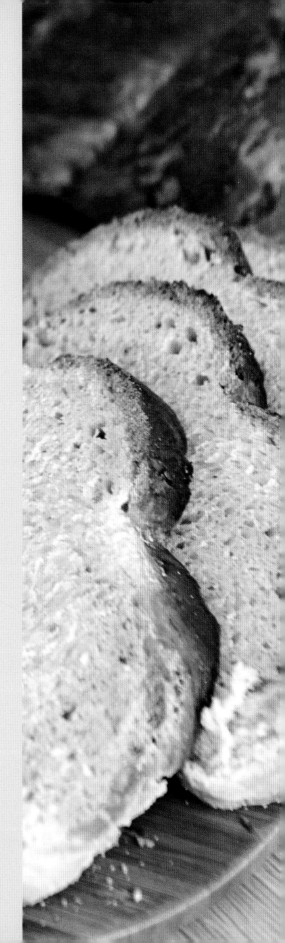

# CHART SYMBOLS

Take the time to learn how to read knitting charts and symbols. Charts are read from right to left on the right side and from left to right on the wrong side, unless otherwise specified. Each square on the chart corresponds to one stitch and the entire chart is made so you'll have an indication of what the finished result will look like.

Many of the symbol abbreviations look complex, but they have a meaning. For example, C4B means a cable worked over four stitches that are crossed with two of the stitches held to the back of the piece.

Or, C6pF means a cable over six stitches with knit and purl stitches, with the cable needle held to the front of the piece.

## Common Symbols

| | |
|---|---|
| ☐ | Knit on RS, purl on WS |
| ⊞ | Knit on RS, knit on WS |
| ⊠ | Purl on RS, knit on WS |
| ◩ | K1tbl (twisted knit) on RS, p1tbl on WS |
| ◩ | Sl 1, k1, psso = slip 1 st knitwise, k1, psso OR work as ssk |
| ◪ | K2tog |
| ◎ | Yarnover |
| ◩ | K2tog tbl |

---

# QR CODES

Each cable symbol has its own QR code (quick response code). When you scan the codes, you will be linked directly to a video on YouTube.com that shows you how to work the technique. These are the author's own recordings, and the resolution on the videos is formatted for a small screen. We recommend that you look at them on your smart phone. A QR code reader can be downloaded for free from your phone's app store. If you don't have a mobile device, just visit the author's YouTube channel (youtube/channel/ UCaPMI5nYl8JjQcHQFN-Mc9Vw) and select the video you want to watch out of the list of uploads. Or simply search YouTube for "Denise Samson" and choose the first result.

Sl 1 twisted (Sl 1 Tw) = Sl 1 tbl, yo, k1, pass the slipped st over 2 sts (1 yo and 1 knit).

C2F = Sl 1 st to cn and hold in front of work, k1, k1 from cn. Alternatively: Insert needle into back of 2nd st on left needle and knit; knit 1st st and slip both sts from needle.

C2B = Sl 1 st to cn and hold in back of work, k1, k1 from cn. Alternatively: Insert needle into 2nd st on left needle and knit; knit 1st st and slip both sts from needle.

Tw1R = K2tog without slipping sts from left needle, insert needle between the sts and k1. Slip both sts from needle.

Tw1L = Insert needle into 2nd st tbl without slipping st from needle, k1, knit both sts through back loops. Slip both sts from needle.

 C2BTw Rib = Sl 1 st to cn and hold in back of work, k1tbl, p1 from cn.

Tw1pL = Sl 1 st to cn and hold in back of work, p1, p1 from cn.

 C2FTw Rib = Sl 1 st to cn and hold in front of work, p1, k1tbl from cn.

Tw1pR = Sl 1 st to cn and hold in front of work, p1, p1 from cn.

 C3B = Sl 1 st to cn and hold in back of work, k2, k1 from cn.
Alternatively: Insert needle into 2nd st on left needle, knit the 2nd, 3rd, and then 1st sts; slip all sts from needle.

 Tw2L = Sl 1 st to cn and hold in front of work, k1tbl, k1tbl from cn.

C3F = Sl 2 sts to cn and hold in front of work, k1, k2 from cn.
Alternatively: Insert needle tbl of 3rd st on left needle, knit the 3rd, 1st and 2nd sts; slip all sts from needle.

 Tw2R = Sl 1 st to cn and hold in back of work, k1tbl, k1tbl from cn.

 C3Bp = Sl 1 st to cn and hold in back of work, k2, p1 from cn.

C3Fp = Sl 2 sts to cn and hold in front of work, p1, k2 from cn.

 C4F = Sl 2 sts to cn and hold in front of work, k2, k2 from cn. Alternatively: Knit the 3rd and 4th sts tbl, knit the 1st and 2nd sts, slip all sts from left needle.

 Wr3 = Sl 3 sts to cn and hold in front of work; wind the yarn clockwise twice around the sts held on cn. Sl the 3 sts to right needle without knitting them.

 C4B = Sl 2 sts to cn and hold in back of work, k2, k2 from cn. Alternatively: Knit the 3rd and 4th sts, knit the 1st and 2nd sts, slip all sts from left needle.

 C2/1L = Sl 1 st to cn and hold in front of work, k2, k1 from cn. Alternatively: Knit the 2nd and 3rd sts on left needle without slipping them from needle, knit 1st st, slip sts to right needle.

 C4Bp = Sl 1 purl st to cn and hold in back of work, k3, p1 from cn.

 C1/2R = Sl 2 sts to cn and hold in back of work, k1, k2 from cn. Alternatively: Knit 3rd st on left needle and then knit the 1st and 2nd sts; slip sts to right needle.

 C4Fp = Sl knit 3 sts to cn and hold in front of work, p1, k3 from cn.

 C4F2p = Sl 2 knit sts to cn and hold in front of work, p2, k2 from cn.

 C3FTw Rib = Sl 2 sts to cn and hold in front of work, k1tbl, place 1 st back on left needle and p1, k1tbl from cn.

C4B2p = Sl 2 purl sts to cn and hold in back of work, k2, p2 from cn.

Cr5 = Sl 2 knit sts and 1 purl st to cn and hold in front of work, k2, sl the purl st on cn back to left needle and purl it; knit the last 2 sts on cn.

C4pF = Sl 1 knit and 2 purl sts to cn and hold in front of work, k1, sl the two purl sts back onto left needle and purl, knit the last st from cn.

C6F = Sl 3 sts to cn and hold in front of work, k3, k3 from cn.

C1/3R = Sl 3 sts to cn and hold in back of work, k1, k3 from cn. Alternatively: Knit the 4th st on left needle without slipping it off needle; now knit the 1st, 2nd, and 3rd sts; slip all 4 sts to right needle.

C6B = Sl 3 sts to cn and hold in back of work, k3, k3 from cn.

C3/1L = Sl 1 st to cn and hold in front of work, k3, k1 from cn. Alternatively: Through back loops, knit the 2nd, 3rd, and 4th sts on left needle with slipping sts from needle, knit the 1st st and slip all 4 sts to right needle.

C6pF = Sl 2 knit sts and 2 purl sts to cn and hold in front of work, k2; sl the 2 purl sts back to left needle and purl them; k2 from cn.

Wr4 = Sl 4 sts to cn and hold in front of work. Wrap the yarn clock-wise 2 times around the sts; slide the sts to right needle without knitting them.

C6pB = Sl 2 knit sts and 2 purl sts to cn and hold in back of work, k2; sl the 2 purl sts back to left needle and purl them, k2 from cn.

C6Bp = Sl 1 purl st to cn and hold in back of work, k5, p1 from cn.

C8F Rib = Sl 4 sts to cn and hold in front of work, k2, p2; k2, p2 from cn.

C6Fp = Sl 5 knit sts to cn and hold in front of work, p1, k5 from cn.

C9pF = Sl 3 sts to cn and hold in front of work, sl 3 sts to a second cn and hold in back of work, k3; k3 from back cn, k3 from front cn.

C7FTw Rib = Sl 3 sts to cn and hold in front of work, k1tbl, p1, k1tbl, p1, from cn: k1tbl, p1, k1tbl.

C9B = Sl 3 sts to cn and hold in back of work, sl 3 sts to another cn and hold in front of work, k3; k3 from front cn, k3 from back cn.

C8B = Sl 4 sts to cn and hold in back of work, k4, k4 from cn.

C9F = Sl 3 sts to cn and hold in front of work, sl 3 sts to another cn and hold in back of work, k3; k3 from back cn, k3 from front cn.

C8F = Sl 4 sts to cn and hold in front of work, k4, k4 from cn.

C10B = Sl 5 sts to cn and hold in back of work, k5, k5 from cn.

C10F = Sl 5 sts to cn and hold in front of work, k5, k5 from cn.

C12B = Sl 6 sts to cn and hold in back of work, k6, k6 from cn.

C12F = Sl 6 sts to cn and hold in front of work, k6, k6 from cn.

C24F Rib = Sl 12 sts to cn and hold in front of work, work (k2, p2) 3 times; from cn, work (k2, p2) 3 times.

C24B Rib = Sl 12 sts to cn and hold in back of work, work (k2, p2) 3 times; from cn, work (k2, p2) 3 times.

C18F Rib = Sl 6 sts to cn and hold in front of work, work (k1, p1) 3 times; from cn, work (k1, p1) 3 times, work last 6 sts as (k1, p1) 3 times.

C18B Rib = Work (k1, p1) 3 times, sl 6 sts to cn and hold in back of work, work (k1, p1) 3 times; from cn, work (k1, p1) 3 times.

## Abbreviations

| | |
|---|---|
| BO | bind off (=British cast off) |
| ch | chain |
| cm | centimeter(s) |
| cn | cable needle |
| CO | cast on |
| cr | cross |
| dc | double crochet (= British treble crochet) |
| dpn | double-pointed needle(s) |
| in | inch(es) |
| k | knit |
| k1f&b | knit into front and then back of same st = 1 st increased |
| k2tog | knit 2 together (right-leaning decrease) |
| mm | millimeters |
| p | purl |
| p2tog | purl 2 together |
| pm | place marker |
| rem | remain(s)(ing) |
| rep | repeat |
| rnd(s) | round(s) |
| RS | right side |
| sc | single crochet (= British double crochet) |
| sl | slip |
| slm | slip marker |
| st(s) | stitch(es) |
| tbl | through back loop(s) |
| tw | twist |
| tw sl | twisted slip stitch |
| wyb | with yarn held in back |
| wyf | with yarn held in front |
| WS | wrong side |
| yo | yarnover |

three-needle bind-off = holding two sets of sts parallel, bind off as follows: Knit together 1st st of each needle; *k2tog with a st from each needle; pass 1st st on right needle over new st*. Rep * to * until all sts have been bound-off.

# CABLE PATTERNS

## PART 1

In this section of the book, I've collected 50 different cable patterns that are shown with symbols, written instructions, and charts. Most of the swatches were worked with 40 stitches and 40 rows. All the swatches were knitted with Lerke from Dale of Norway on U.S. size 6 / 4 mm needles. Some of these cables are used in the patterns in the second part of the book, so you can see how the various cable techniques look when they are worked over a larger surface. You can also see how the cables look with finer or heavier yarn, different sizes of needles, or how several cable patterns can be combined in a garment or other type of knitting.

I hope you'll be inspired to try all kinds of cables in your own work, and become just as hooked on cables as I am.

Good luck!

# False Cables

These are cables worked with two needles and no cable needle. The motifs are quick to knit and make a raised structure. They are fine on their own, but can also be used in combination with more complex types of cables.

# NO. 1 FALSE CABLE

### QR code: Sl 1 twisted

This pattern is worked without the use of a cable needle. The cable chart shows five repeats across. One cable repeat is worked over 4 stitches and 4 rows. The pattern is used for the Men's Aran Sweater on page 162 and the Women's Aran Wrap Sweater on page 160.

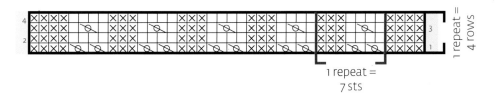

1 repeat = 4 rows

1 repeat = 7 sts

CO 40 sts.

**Row 1:** P4, *(Sl 1 Tw) 2 times, p3*; rep * to * 3 more times, (Sl 1 Tw) 2 times, p4.
**Row 2:** K4, (p4, k3) 4 times, p4, k4.
**Row 3:** P4, (k1, Sl 1 Tw, k1, p3) 4 times, k1, Sl 1 Tw, k1, p4.
**Row 4:** Work as for Row 2.

Rep Rows 1-4 9 more times = 40 rows.

☐ Knit on RS, purl on WS

☒ Purl on RS, knit on WS

⧄ Sl 1 Tw = Sl 1 st tbl, yo, k1, psso
(pass slipped st over the yo and k1)

# NO. 2 SLIPPED CABLE TO THE RIGHT

**QR code: C1/3R**

You can work this motif without a cable needle. The repeat is 12 stitches and 8 rows in stockinette. The pattern is worked by crossing 1 stitch over 3 to the right. The pattern is used for the Throw on page 128.

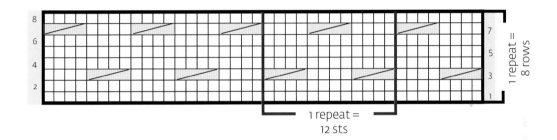

1 repeat = 12 sts

1 repeat = 8 rows

CO 40 sts.

**Row 1:** Knit.
**Row 2 and all WS rows:** Purl.
**Row 3:** (C1/3R, k4) 5 times.
**Row 5:** Knit.
**Row 7:** (K4, C1/3R) 5 times.
**Row 8:** Purl.

Rep Rows 1–8 4 more times = 40 rows.

☐ Knit on RS, purl on WS

▱ C1/3R = Sl 3 sts to cn and hold in back of work, k1, k3 from cn
Alternatively: Knit the 4th st on left needle but do not remove st, knit the 1st, 2nd, and 3rd sts, slip all 4 sts onto right needle

# NO. 3 SLIPPED CABLE
# TO THE LEFT

**QR code: C3/1L**
You can work this motif without a cable needle. The repeat is 12 stitches and 8 rows in stockinette. The pattern is worked by crossing 1 stitch over 3 to the left. The pattern is used for the Throw, page 128.

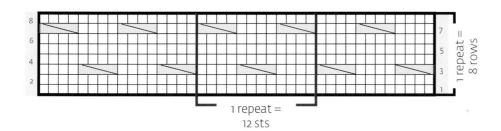

1 repeat =
12 sts

1 repeat =
8 rows

CO 40 sts.

**Row 1:** Knit.
**Row 2 and all WS rows:** Purl.
**Row 3:** (C3/1L, k4) 5 times.
**Row 5:** Knit.
**Row 7:** (K4, C3/1L) 5 times.
**Row 8:** Purl.

Rep Rows 1-8 4 more times = 40 rows.

☐  Knit on RS, purl on WS

▱  C3/1L = Sl 1 to cn and hold in front of work, k3, k1 from cn. Alternatively: Knit the 2nd, 3rd, and 4th sts on left needle through back loops without dropping them off needle, k1 and slip all 4 sts over to right needle

# NO. 4  OPTIC EFFECT CABLE

---

**QR codes: Tw1R and Tw1L**

This cable is worked over 36 stitches and 28 rows. You don't need a cable needle. This is a good cable for large items, such as a sweater, blanket, or bathmat, where the pattern can be repeated several times. In this case, I've knitted garter stitch edges to showcase the pattern.

The pattern is used on the Potholders, page 122.

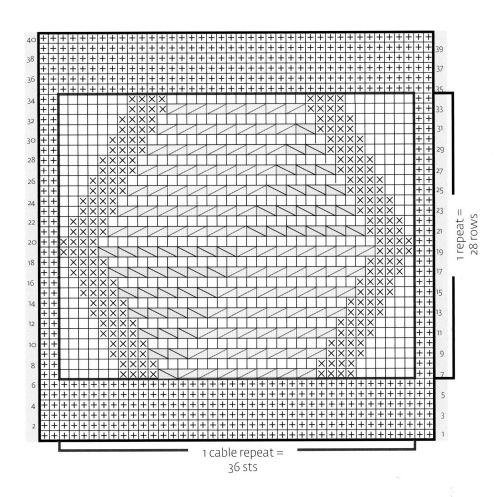

1 repeat = 28 rows

1 cable repeat = 36 sts

CO 40 sts.

**Rows 1-6:** Knit.
**Row 7:** K8, p4, (Tw1R) 7 times, Tw1L, p4, k8.
**Row 8:** K2, p6, k4, p16, k4, p6, k2.
**Row 9:** K7, p4, (Tw1R) 7 times, (Tw1L) 2 times, p4, k7.
**Row 10:** K2, p5, k4, p18, k4, p5, k2.
**Row 11:** K6, p4, (Tw1R) 7 times, (Tw1L) 3 times, p4, k6.
**Row 12:** K2, p4, k4, p20, k4, p4, k2.
**Row 13:** K5, p4, (Tw1R) 7 times, (Tw1L) 4 times, p4, k5.
**Row 14:** K2, p3, k4, p22, k4, p3, k2.
**Row 15:** K4, p4, (Tw1R) 7 times, (Tw1L) 5 times, p4, k4.
**Row 16:** K2, p2, k4, p24, k4, p2, k2.
**Row 17:** K3, p4, (Tw1R) 7 times, (Tw1L) 6 times, p4, k3.
**Row 18:** K2, p1, k4, p26, k4, p1, k2.
**Row 19:** K2, p4, (Tw1R) 7 times, (Tw1L) 7 times, p4, k2.
**Row 20:** K6, p28, k6.
**Row 21:** K3, p4, (Tw1L) 6 times, (Tw1R) 7 times, p4, k3.
**Row 22:** K2, p1, k4, p26, k4, p1, k2.
**Row 23:** K4, p4, (Tw1L) 5 times, (Tw1R) 7 times, p4, k4.
**Row 24:** K2, p2, k4, p24, k4, p2, k2.
**Row 25:** K5, p4, (Tw1L) 4 times, (Tw1R) 7 times, p4, k5.
**Row 26:** K2, p3, k4, p22, k4, p3, k2.
**Row 27:** K6, p4, (Tw1L) 3 times, (Tw1R) 7 times, p4, k6.

**Row 28:** K2, p4, k4, p20, k4, p4, k2.
**Row 29:** K7, p4, (Tw1L) 2 times, (Tw1R) 7 times, p4, k7.
**Row 30:** K2, p5, k4, p18, k4, p5, k2.
**Row 31:** K8, p4, Tw1L, (Tw1R) 7 times, p4, k8.
**Row 32:** K2, p6, k4, p16, k4, p6, k2.
**Row 33:** K9, p4, (Tw1R) 7 times, p4, k9.
**Row 34:** K2, p7, k4, p14, k4, p7, k2.
**Rows 35-40:** Knit.

| | |
|---|---|
| ⊞ | Knit on RS, knit on WS |
| ☐ | Knit on RS, purl on WS |
| ⊠ | Purl on RS, knit on WS |
| ⟋ | Tw1R= K2tog but do not drop from needle, insert needle between the 2 sts and knit the 1st st. Sl both sts from needle |
| ⟍ | Tw1L= Knit 2nd st on left needle tbl but do not drop from needle, knit 1st and 2nd sts tog tbl. Sl both sts from needle |

On the following pages, you will learn how to knit narrow cables, wide cables, cables that lean to the right and to the left, and that are worked with or without a cable needle. Most of the patterns are worked on a reverse stockinette background so the cable pattern will be as distinct as possible.

# NO. 5  SIMPLE DIAGONAL CABLE

**QR code: C2B**

This cable design shows five identical repeats. One repeat of the cable is worked over 6 stitches and 10 rows. You can work the cables with or without a cable needle.

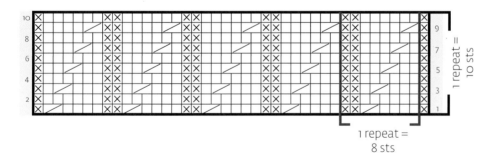

1 repeat = 10 sts

1 repeat = 8 sts

CO 40 sts.

Rep Rows 1-10 3 more times = 40 rows.

**Row 1:** P1 (k4, C2B, p2) 4 times, k4, C2B, p1.
**Row 2 and all WS rows:** K1, p6, (k2, p6) 4 times, k1.
**Row 3:** P1, (k3, C2B, k1, p2) 4 times, k3, C2B, k1, p1.
**Row 5:** P1, (k2, C2B, k2, p2) 4 times, k2, C2B, k2, p1.
**Row 7:** P1, (k1, C2B, k3, p2) 4 times, k1, C2B, k3, p1.
**Row 9:** P1, (C2B, k4, p2) 4 times, C2B, k4, p1.
**Row 10:** K1, p6, (k2, p6) 4 times, k1.

☐ Knit on RS, purl on WS

☒ Purl on RS, knit on WS

▱ C2B = Sl 1 st to cn and hold in back of work, k1, k1 from cn

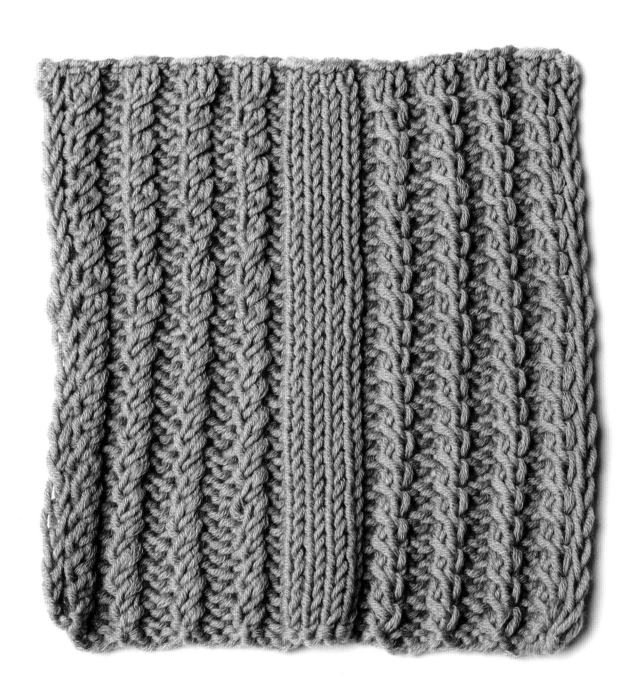

# NO. 6  LITTLE BABY CABLE

**QR codes: C2F and C2B**

This swatch features cables worked over 2 sts and 2 rows. The pattern on the right side of the swatch has four identical cables that lean to the left and the pattern on the left has four identical cables leaning to the right. Both patterns work well as edges for a sweater, or the small cables can be combined with larger cables. You can work the cables with or without a cable needle. Both cables are worked on the Men's Aran Sweater on page 162, as well as on the Women's Aran Wrap Sweater on page 160 and the Hat, Cowl, Mittens, and Leg Warmer set (page 132).

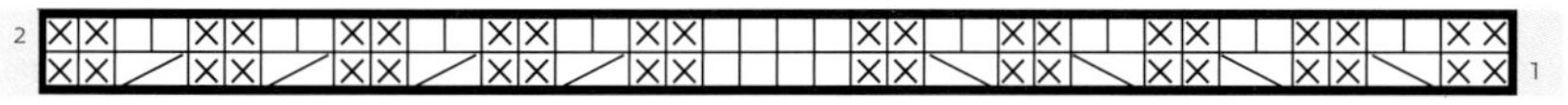

CO 40 sts.

**Row 1:** (P2, C2F) 4 times, p2, k4, p2, (C2B, p2) 4 times.
**Row 2:** (K2, p2) 4 times, k2, p4, k2, (p2, k2) 4 times.

Rep Rows 1-2 19 more times = 40 rows.

□  Knit on RS, purl on WS

☒  Purl on RS, knit on WS

◺  C2F = Sl 1 st to cn and hold in front of work, k1, k1 from cn

◹  C2B = Sl 1 st to cn and hold in back of work, k1, k1 from cn

# NO. 7 EASY CABLE

---

**QR codes: C2F and C2B**

This pattern is worked the same way as for the Little Baby Cable on page 26, but instead of working only one row between the cables, there are five rows between each. The cable repeat is 2 stitches and 6 rows, rather than 2 stitches and 2 rows. This gives the cable a completely different look. The swatch shows four identical cables that lean to the left and four identical cables leaning to the right. The pattern is used for Sigrid's Poncho (see page 150).

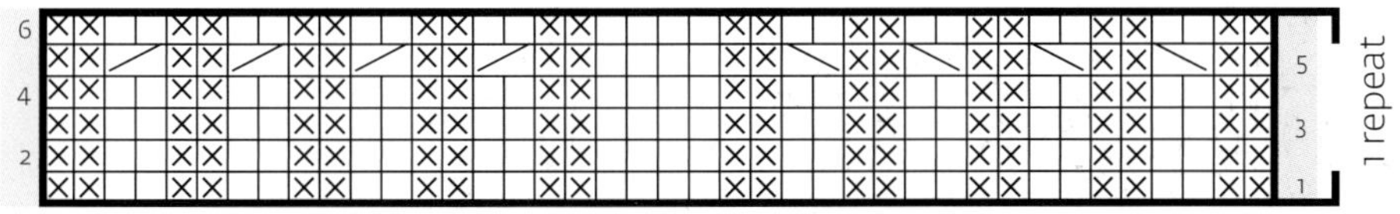

CO 40 sts.

**Row 1:** (P2, k2) 4 times, p2, k4, p2, (k2, p2) 4 times.
**Row 2 and all WS rows:** (K2, p2) 4 times, k2, p4, k2, (p2, k2) 4 times.
**Row 3:** Work as for Row 1.
**Row 5:** (P2, C2F) 4 times, p2, k4, p2, (C2B, p2) 4 times.
**Row 6:** (K2, p2) 4 times, k2, p4, k2, (p2, k2) 4 times.

Rep Rows 1-6 6 more times and then work Rows 1-4 = 40 rows.

☐  Knit on RS, purl on WS

☒  Purl on RS, knit on WS

▱  C2F = Sl 1 st to cn and hold in front of work, k1, k1 from cn

▱  C2B = Sl 1 st to cn and hold in back of work, k1, k1 from cn

# NO. 8  WIDE BABY CABLE

**QR code: C1/2R**

This pattern is worked as for the Little Baby Cable on page 26, but the cable is worked over 3 instead of 2 stitches. The swatch has seven identical cables across. The technique is the same as for the slipped cable on page 18. If you want to cross the cable in the opposite direction, see the cable pattern on page 20 and cross the stitches to the left.

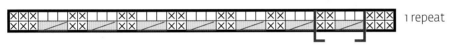

1 repeat

1 repeat = 5 sts

CO 39 sts.

**Row 1:** P3, (C1/2R, p2) 6 times, C1/2R, p3.
**Row 2:** K3, (p3, k2) 6 times, p3, k3.

Rep Rows 1-2 19 more times = 40 rows.

☐ Knit on RS, purl on WS

☒ Purl on RS, knit on WS

▨ C1/2R = Sl 2 sts to cn and hold in back of work, k1, k2 from cn

# NO. 9 ROPE

## QR codes: C4F and C4B

The swatch features three identical cables leaning to the left with a repeat of 4 stitches and 4 rows. The left side of the swatch shows three identical cables leaning to the right. Both cables are used on the Hat, Cowl, Mittens, and Leg Warmer set on page 132.

CO 40 sts.

**Row 1:** (P2, k4) 3 times, p4, (k4, p2) 3 times.
**Row 2:** (K2, p4) 3 times, k4, (p4, k2) 3 times.
**Row 3:** (P2, C4F) 3 times, p4, (C4B, p2) 3 times.
**Row 4:** K2, p4) 3 times, k4, (p4, k2) 3 times.

Rep Rows 1-4 9 more times = 40 rows.

☐ Knit on RS, purl on WS

☒ Purl on RS, knit on WS

C4F = Sl 2 sts to cn and hold in front of work, k2, k2 from cn

C4B = Sl 2 sts to cn and hold in back of work, k2, k2 from cn

# NO. 10 NAUTICAL CABLE

**QR code: C4F**

The six identical 4-stitch wide cables on the swatch lean to the left; however, instead of every 4th row, this cable is crossed on every 8th row.

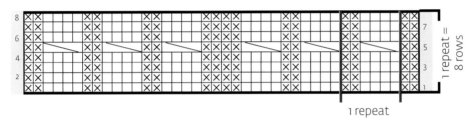

1 repeat

1 repeat = 8 rows

CO 40 sts.

▢ Knit on RS, purl on WS

☒ Purl on RS, knit on WS

◢ C4F = Sl 2 sts to cn and hold in front of work, k2, k2 from cn

**Row 1:** (P2, k4) 3 times, p4, (k4, p2) 3 times.
**Row 2:** (K2, p4) 3 times, k4, (p4, k2) 3 times.
**Row 3:** Work as for Row 1.
**Row 4:** Work as for Row 2.
**Row 5:** (P2, C4F) 3 times, p4, (C4B, p2) 3 times.
**Row 6:** Work as for Row 2.
**Row 7:** Work as for Row 1.
**Row 8:** Work as for Row 2.

Rep Rows 1-8 5 more times = 40 rows.

# NO. 11 HAIR BRAID CABLE

**QR codes: C4F and C4B**

This swatch has four identical cables. The cable crossings alternately lean to the right and to the left on every other row. One cable repeat is 6 stitches and 4 rows and the pattern is used on the Women's Aran Wrap Sweater (see page 160).

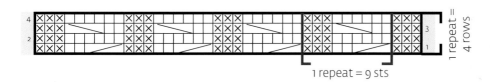

1 repeat = 9 sts

1 repeat = 4 rows

CO 39 sts.

**Row 1:** P3, (C4B, k2, p3) 4 times.
**Row 2:** K3, (p6, k3) 4 times.
**Row 3:** P3, (k2, C4F, p3) 4 times.
**Row 4:** Work as for Row 2.

Rep Rows 1-4 9 more times = 40 rows.

☐   Knit on RS, purl on WS

☒   Purl on RS, knit on WS

▱   C4B = Sl 2 sts to cn and hold in back of work, k2, k2 from cn

▱   C4F = Sl 2 sts to cn and hold in front of work, k2, k2 from cn

# NO. 12 BASKETWEAVE CABLE

**QR codes: C4F and C4B**

Here's a pattern for a tight cable in which the cables cross to the left on the first row and then to the right on the third row. The structure is almost like weaving. The repeat is 10 stitches (= 8 stitches + 2) and 4 rows. This cable is featured on the Boot Toppers (see page 144).

CO 40 sts.

**Row 1:** P3, k2, (C4F) 8 times, p3.
**Row 2:** K3, p34, k3.
**Row 3:** P3, (C4B) 8 times, k2, p3.
**Row 4:** K3, p34, k3.

Rep Rows 1–4 9 more times = 40 rows.

☐  Knit on RS, purl on WS

☒  Purl on RS, knit on WS

⬜  C4F = Sl 2 sts to cn and hold in front of work, k2, k2 from cn

⬜  C4B = Sl 2 sts to cn and hold in back of work, k2, k2 from cn

# NO. 13 HEAVY ROPE CABLE

**QR codes: C6F and C6B**

The swatch shows two cables leaning to the left and two leaning to the right. The cable repeat is worked over 6 stitches and 6 rows.

CO 40 sts.

**Row 1:** P2, (k6, p4) 3 times, k6, p2.
**Row 2 and all WS rows:** K2, (p6, k4) 3 times, p6, k2.
**Row 3:** P2, C6F, p4, C4F, p4, C6B, p4, C6B, p2.
**Row 5:** Work as for Row 1.
**Row 6:** Work as for Row 2.

Rep Rows 1-6 5 more times and then work Rows 1-4 = 40 rows.

☐ Knit on RS, purl on WS

☒ Purl on RS, knit on WS

C6F = Sl 3 sts to cn and hold in front of work, k3, k3 from cn

C6B = Sl 3 sts to cn and hold in back of work, k3, k3 from cn

# NO. 14 CLIMBING CABLE

**QR codes: C4F and C4B**

This pattern features cables that cross to both the right and the left over a stockinette background. The repeat is 12 sts + 2 and 8 rows. It's used for the Breakfast Mats (see page 120).

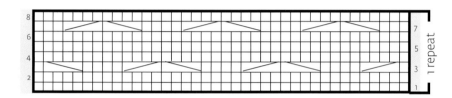

CO 38 sts.

**Row 1:** Knit.
**Row 2 and all WS rows:** Purl.
**Row 3:** K1, C4B, (k4, C4F, C4B) 2 times, k4, C4F, k1.
**Row 5:** Knit.
**Row 7:** K3, C4F, C4B, (k4, C4F, C4B) 2 times, k3.
**Row 8:** Purl.

Rep Rows 1-8 4 more times = 40 rows.

☐ Knit on RS, purl on WS

C4F = Sl 2 sts to cn and hold in front of work, k2, k2 from cn

C4B = Sl 2 sts to cn and hold in back of work, k2, k2 from cn

# NO. 15 DOUBLE CABLE

**QR codes: C4F and C4B**

This swatch shows three identical cables with each cable actually consisting of two abutting cables. A 4-stitch cable leans to the right and its mate leans to the left. The complete cable pattern repeats over 12 stitches and 6 rows. It's used for the Men's Aran Sweater (see page 162).

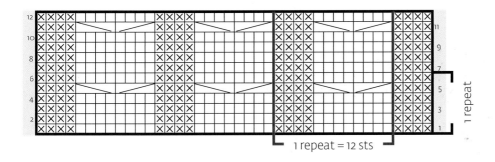

1 repeat = 12 sts

CO 40 sts.

**Row 1:** P4, (k8, p4) 3 times.
**Row 2 and all WS rows:** K4, (p8, k4) 3 times.
**Row 3:** Work as for Row 1.
**Row 5:** P4, (C4B, C4F, p4) 3 times.
**Rows 6-10:** Work as for Rows 1-2.
**Row 11:** Work as for Row 5.
**Row 12:** Work as for Row 2.

Rep Rows 1-12 twice more and then work Rows 1-4 = 40 rows.

☐   Knit on RS, purl on WS

☒   Purl on RS, knit on WS

C4B = Sl 2 sts to cn and hold in back of work, k2, k2 from cn

C4F = Sl 2 sts to cn and hold in front of work, k2, k2 from cn

# NO. 16 WIDE HAIR BRAID CABLE

**QR codes: C8F and C8B**

This pattern shows two identical cables that lean to both the right and left. The repeat is worked over 12 stitches and 16 rows. The pattern is used on the Women's Aran Wrap Sweater (see page 160).

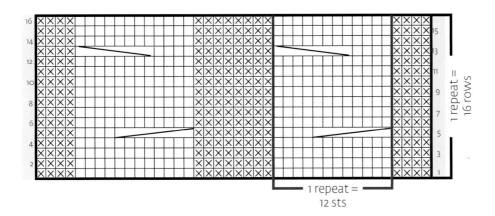

CO 40 sts.

**Row 1 and all RS rows without cable crossing:** P4, k12, p8, k12, p4.
**Row 2 and all WS rows:** K4, p12, k8, p12, k4.
**Row 3:** Work as for Row 1.
**Row 5:** P4, C8B, k4, p8, C8B, k4, p4.
**Row 13:** P4, k4, C8F, p8, k4, C8F, p4.
**Rows 14-16:** Work as for Rows 1-2.

Rep Rows 1-16 once more and then work Rows 1-8 = 40 rows.

|  | Knit on RS, purl on WS |
|---|---|
| ⊠ | Purl on RS, knit on WS |
|  | C8B = Sl 4 sts to cn and hold in back of work, k4, k4 from cn |
|  | C8F = Sl 4 sts to cn and hold in front of work, k4, k4 from cn |

# NO. 17  WIDE NAUTICAL CABLE

**QR codes: C12F and C12B**
This swatch shows one cable leaning to the right and the other to the left. The repeat is worked over 12 stitches and 16 rows. The pattern is used for the Cowl set—the left-leaning cable is on the left mitten and leg warmer and the right-leaning cable appears on the right mitten and leg warmer (see pages 132-135).

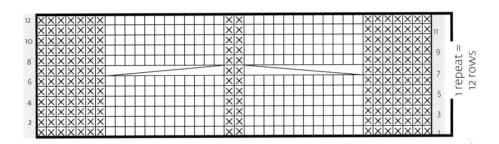

CO 40 sts.

**Rows 1, 3, and 5:** P7, k12, p2, k12, p7.
**Row 2 and all WS rows:** K7, p12, k2, p12, k7.
**Row 7:** P7, (C12F, p2, C12B, p7.
**Rows 9-12:** Work as for Rows 1-2.

Rep Rows 1-12 twice more and then work Rows 1-4 = 40 rows.

| | |
|---|---|
| ☐ | Knit on RS, purl on WS |
| ☒ | Purl on RS, knit on WS |
| ⬛ | C12F = Sl 6 sts to cn and hold in front of work, k6, k6 from cn |
| ⬛ | C12B = Sl 6 sts to cn and hold in back of work, k6, k6 from cn |

# NO. 18 TWIN CABLE

**QR codes: C10F and C10B**
This pattern shows two identical cables that first lean to the left on one row and then to the right on a later row. The repeat is worked over 32 stitches and 12 rows. You can divide the pattern repeat in two so that you only work the first 16 stitches for one large cable. The pattern is used on the Bag (see page 168).

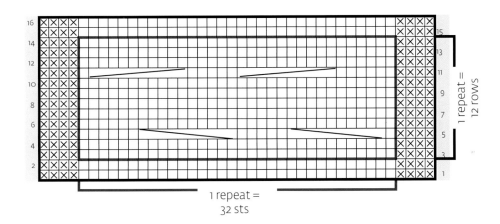

1 repeat =
32 sts

1 repeat =
12 rows

CO 40 sts.

**Rows 1 and 3**: P4, k32, p4.
**Row 2 and all WS rows:** K4, p32, k4.
**Row 5:** P4, k1, C10F, k5, C10F, k6, p4.
**Row 7:** P4, k32, p4.
**Row 9:** P4, k32, p4.
**Row 11:** K4, k6, C10B, k5, C10B, k1, p4.
**Row 13:** P4, k32, p4.
**Row 14:** K4, p32, k4.

Rep Rows 3-14 twice more and
then work Rows 15-16 = 40 rows.

**Row 15:** P4, k32, p4.
**Row 16:** K4, p32, k4.

☐ Knit on RS, purl on WS

☒ Purl on RS, knit on WS

C10F = Sl 5 sts to cn and hold in front of work,
k5, k5 from cn

C10B = Sl 5 sts to cn and hold in back of work,
k5, k5 from cn

# NO. 19 PINEAPPLE CABLE

**QR code: C2F**

This cable pattern has a repeat of 8 stitches and 12 rows. By repeating it over a larger cable, you produce a pretty pattern. The pattern is used on the Pullover for Petter (see page 152).

CO 40 sts.

**Rows 1, 3, and 5:** P2, (k4, p1, C2F, p1) 4 times, k4, p2.
**Rows 2, 4, and 6:** K2, (p4, k1, C2F, k1) 4 times, p4, k2.
**Row 7:** P2, (p1, C2F, p1, k4) 4 times, p1, C2F, p3.
**Row 8:** K2, (k1, C2F, k1, p4) 4 times, k1, C2F, k3.
**Rows 9 and 11:** Work as for Row 7.
**Rows 10 and 12:** Work as for Row 8.

Rep Rows 1–12 twice more and then work Rows 1–4 = 40 rows.

☐   Knit on RS, purl on WS

☒   Purl on RS, knit on WS

⬡   C2F = *on RS*: Sl 1 st to cn and hold in front of work, k1, k1 from cn
*on WS*: Sl 1 st to cn and hold in front of work, p1, p1 from cn

# NO. 20 SIDEWINDER CABLE

**QR codes: Tw1pL, Tw1pR, C2/1L, C2/1R**

There are four different cable crossings in this pattern. This cable pattern repeats with 12 stitches and 12 rows. By repeating it over a larger cable, you produce a pretty pattern. The pattern is used for Tormod's Stockings (see page 148).

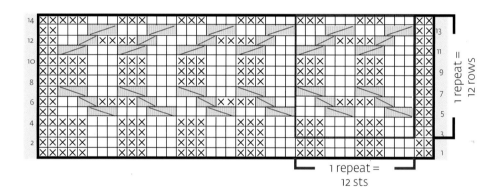

1 repeat = 12 rows

1 repeat = 12 sts

CO 40 sts.

**Rows 1 and 3:** P2, (k3, p3) 6 times, p2.
**Rows 2 and 4:** K5 (p3, k3) 5 times, p3, k2.
**Row 5:** P2, (C2/1L, k3) 6 times, p2.
**Row 6:** K2, p2, (Tw1pR, k4, Tw1pR, p4) 2 times, Tw1pR, k4, Tw1pR, p2, k2.
**Row 7:** P2, (k3, C2/1L) 6 times, p2.
**Rows 8-10:** Work as for Rows 1-3.
**Row 11:** P2, (k3, C1/2R) 6 times, p2.
**Row 12:** K2, p2, (Tw1pL, k4, Tw1pL, p4) 2 times, Tw1pL, k4, Tw1pL, p2, k2.
**Row 13:** P2, (C1/2R, k3) 6 times, p2.
**Row 14:** K5, (p3, k3) 5 times, p3, k2.

Rep Rows 3-14 twice more and then work Rows 1-2 = 40 rows.

|  |  |
|---|---|
| ☐ | Knit on RS, purl on WS |
| ☒ | Purl on RS, knit on WS |
| ◩ | Tw1pL = Sl 1 st to cn and hold in back of work, p1, p1 from cn |
| ◪ | Tw1pR = Sl 1 st to cn and hold in front of work, p1, p1 from cn |
| ◩ | C2/1L = Sl 1 st to cn and hold in front of work, k2, k1 from cn |
| ◪ | C1/2R = Sl 2 sts to cn and hold in back of work, k1, k2 from cn |

# NO. 21 KNOT CABLES

**QR codes: C4F and C4B**

This swatch shows three identical cables with each cable leaning both right and left as for the pattern on page 38. The pattern repeats over 8 stitches and 20 rows.

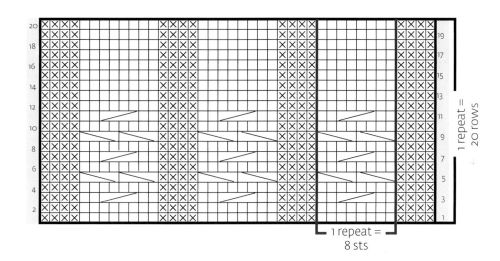

1 repeat =
20 rows

1 repeat =
8 sts

CO 40 sts.

**Row 1:** (P4, k8) 3 times, p4.
**Row 2 and all WS rows:** (K4, p8) 3 times, k4.
**Row 3:** (P4, k2, C4B, k2) 3 times, p4.
**Row 5:** (P4, C4F, C4B) 3 times, p4.
**Row 7:** Work as for Row 3.
**Row 9:** Work as for Row 5.
**Row 11:** Work as for Row 3.
**Rows 12-20:** Work as for Rows 1-2.

Rep Rows 1-20 once more = 40 rows.

☐ Knit on RS, purl on WS

☒ Purl on RS, knit on WS

C4F = Sl 2 sts to cn and hold in front of work, k2, k2 from cn

C4B = Sl 2 sts to cn and hold in back of work, k2, k2 from cn

# NO. 22 DIAGONAL KNOTS

**QR code: C6F**

This swatch shows two pairs of cables that stagger diagonally to the left. The pattern repeat is 14 stitches and 20 rows and it's used on the Carpenter's Comforts (see page 139).

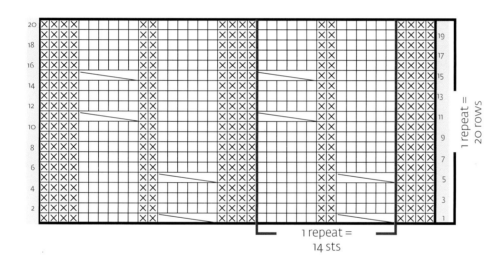

CO 40 sts.

**Row 1:** (P4, C6F, p2, k6) 2 times, p4.
**Row 2 and all WS rows:** K4, (p6, k2, p6, k4) 2 times.
**Row 3:** (P4, k6, p2, k6) 2 times, p4.
**Row 5:** Work as for Row 1.
**Rows 7 and 9:** Work as for Row 3.
**Row 11:** (P4, k6, p2, C6F) 2 times, p4.
**Row 13:** Work as for Row 3.
**Row 15:** Work as for Row 11.
**Rows 17 and 19:** Work as for Row 3.
**Row 20:** K4, (p6, k2, p6, k4) 2 times.

Rep Rows 1–20 once more = 40 rows.

☐ Knit on RS, purl on WS

☒ Purl on RS, knit on WS

▱ C6F = Sl 3 sts to cn and hold in front of work, k3, k3 from cn

# NO. 23 XO-CABLE

**QR codes: C4F and C4B**

This swatch shows three identical cables with each cable leaning both right and left. It is called an XO-cable because the motif clearly resembles an X and an O. The pattern repeats over 12 stitches and 16 rows.

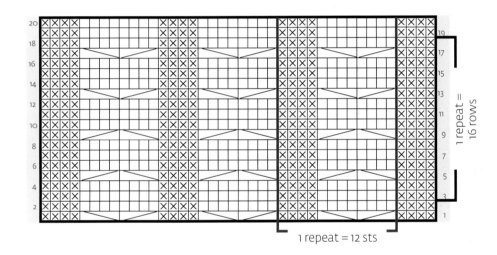

1 repeat = 16 rows

1 repeat = 12 sts

CO 40 sts.

**Row 1:** P4, (C4B, C4F, p4) 3 times.
**Row 2 and all WS rows:** K4, (p8, k4) 3 times.
**Row 3:** P4, (k8, p4) 3 times.
**Row 5:** P4, (C4F, C4B, p4) 3 times.
**Row 7:** P4, (k8, p4) 3 times.
**Row 9:** P4, (C4F, C4B, p4) 3 times.
**Row 11:** P4, k8, p4) 3 times.
**Row 13:** P4, (C4B, C4F, p4) 3 times.
**Row 15:** P4, (k8, p4) 3 times.
**Row 17:** P4, (C4B, C4F, p4) 3 times.
**Row 18:** K4, (p8, k4) 3 times.

Rep Rows 3-18 once more.

**Row 19:** P4, (k8, p4) 3 times.
**Row 20:** K4, (p8, k4) 3 times.

Rep Rows 1-4 once more = 40 rows.

|   |   |
|---|---|
| ☐ | Knit on RS, purl on WS |
| ☒ | Purl on RS, knit on WS |
|   | C4F = Sl 2 sts to cn and hold in front of work, k2, k2 from cn |
|   | C4B = Sl 2 sts to cn and hold in back of work, k2, k2 from cn |

# NO. 24 BEEHIVE CABLE

**QR codes: C4F and C4B**

This pattern is very similar to the design on page 60. The three cables lean both right and left. The motif is called a beehive cable because the pattern makes a deep impression on the surface. The pattern repeats over 12 stitches and 8 rows.

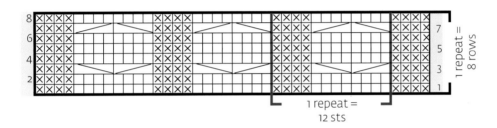

CO 40 sts.

**Row 1:** P4, (k8, p4) 3 times.
**Row 2 and all WS rows:** K4, (p8, k4) 3 times.
**Row 3:** P4, (C4B, C4F, p4) 3 times.
**Row 5:** P4, (k8, p4) 3 times.
**Row 7:** P4, (C4F, C4B, p4) 3 times.
**Row 8:** K4, (p8, k4) 3 times.

Rep Rows 1–8 4 more times = 40 rows.

☐ Knit on RS, purl on WS

☒ Purl on RS, knit on WS

C4F = Sl 2 sts to cn and hold in front of work, k2, k2 from cn

C4B = Sl 2 sts to cn and hold in back of work, k2, k2 from cn

# NO. 25 WAFFLE CABLE

**QR codes: C6F and C6B**

This swatch features one cable combined with cables that lean both right and left. The pattern repeats over 20 stitches and 6 rows. You'll find waffle cables on the Cozy Slippers (see page 126).

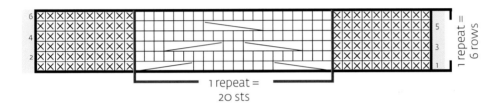

CO 40 sts.

**Row 1:** P10, C6F, k8, C6B, p10.
**Row 2 and all WS rows:** K10, p20, k10.
**Row 3:** P10, k3, C6F, k2, C6B, k3, p10.
**Row 5:** P10, k7, C6F, k7, p10.
**Row 6:** K10, p20, k10.

Rep Rows 1-6 5 more times and then rep Rows 1-4 = 40 rows.

☐ Knit on RS, purl on WS

☒ Purl on RS, knit on WS

C6F = Sl 3 sts to cn and hold in front of work, k3, k3 from cn

C6B = Sl 3 sts to cn and hold in back of work, k3, k3 from cn

# NO. 26 WIDE WHEATEARS CABLE

**QR codes: C4F and C4B**
This pattern swatch has three cables; the center cable is a combination of the cables to its right and left. All three cables can be used separately but go well together in the same pattern repeat. The single cables are worked over 8 stitches and the center cable has 16 stitches. The entire repeat is worked over 36 stitches and 6 rows.

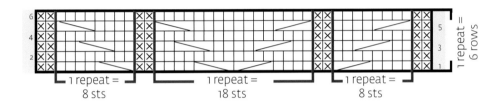

CO 40 sts.

**Row 1:** P2, k4, C4B, p2, k4, C4B, C4F, k4, p2, C4F, k4, p2.
**Row 2 and all WS rows:** K2, p8, k2, p16, k2, p8, k2.
**Row 3:** P2, k2, C4B, k2, p2, k2, C4B, k4, C4F, k2, p2, k2, C4F, k2, p2.
**Row 5:** K2, C4B, k4, p2, C4B, k8, C4F, p2, k4, C4F, p2.
**Row 6:** Work as for Row 2.

Rep Rows 1-6 5 more times and then rep Rows 1-4 = 40 rows.

☐  Knit on RS, purl on WS

☒  Purl on RS, knit on WS

▱  C4F = Sl 2 sts to cn and hold in front of work, k2, k2 from cn

▱  C4B = Sl 2 sts to cn and hold in back of work, k2, k2 from cn

# Diamonds

Diamond motifs are most often worked with a texture-effect pattern inside a diamond—or the diamonds connect with a cable. Reverse stockinette or bobbles combine with diamonds for an exciting effect.

# NO. 27 DIAMOND AND BOBBLES

**QR codes: C3Bp, C3Fp, Cr5, and bobble**

This pattern features diamond cables with bobbles (also called blackberries) in the center of each diamond. The repeat is worked over 10 stitches and 20 rows. You can omit the bobbles and substitute a purl stitch for each bobble instead.

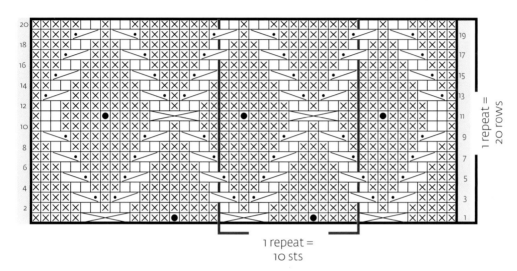

1 repeat =
20 rows

1 repeat =
10 sts

CO 43 sts.

**Row 1:** P5, (Cr5, p4, 1 bobble, p4) 2 times, Cr5, p5.
**Row 2:** K5, (p2, k1, p2, k9) 2 times, p2, k1, p2, k5.
**Row 3:** P4, (C3Bp, p1, C3Fp, p7) 2 times, C3Bp, p1, C3Fp, p4.
**Row 4:** K4, (p2, k3, p2, k7) 2 times, p2, k3, p2, k4.
**Row 5:** P3, (C3Bp, p3, C3Fp, p5) 2 times, C3Bp, p3, C3Fp, p3.
**Row 6:** K3, (p2, k5, p2, k5) 2 times, p2, k5, p2, k3.
**Row 7:** P2, (C3Bp, p5, C3Fp, p3) 2 times, C3Bp, p5, C3Fp, p7.
**Row 8:** K2, (p2, k7, p2, k3) 2 times, p2, k7, p2, k2.
**Row 9:** P1, (C3Bp, p7, C3Fp, p1) 2 times, C3Bp, p7, C3Fp, p1.
**Row 10:** K1, (p2, k9, p2, k1) 2 times, p2, k9, p2, k1.
**Row 11:** P1, k2, (p4, 1 bobble, p4, Cr5) 2 times, p4, 1 bobble, p4, k2, p1.
**Row 12:** K1, (p2, k9, p2, k1) 2 times, p2, k9, p2, k1.
**Row 13:** P1, (C3Fp, p7, C3Bp, p1) 2 times, C3Fp, p7, C3Bp, p1.
**Row 14:** K2, (p2, k7, p2, k3) 2 times, p2, k7, p2, k2.
**Row 15:** P2, (C3Fp, p5, C3Bp, p3) 2 times, C3Fp, p5, C3Bp, p2.
**Row 16:** K3, (p2, k5, p2, k5) 2 times, p2, k5, p2, k3.

**Row 17:** P3, (C3Fp, p3, C3Bp, p5) 2 times, C3Fp, p3, C3Bp, p3.
**Row 18:** K4, (p2, k3, p2, k7) 2 times, p2, k3, p2, k4.
**Row 19:** P4, (C3Fp, p1, C3Bp, p7) 2 times, C3Fp, p1, C3Bp, p4.
**Row 20:** K5, (p2, k1, p2, k9) 2 times, p2, k1, p2, k5.

Rep Rows 1-20 once more = 40 rows.

☐ Knit on RS, purl on WS

☒ Purl on RS, knit on WS

● Bobble = Work (k1, k1tbl, k1, k1tbl, k1) into the same st. Turn, p5; turn, k5; turn, p2tog, p1, p2tog; turn, k3tog (=1 st rem)

⬚ C3Bp = Sl 1 st to cn and hold in back of work, k2, p1 from cn

⬚ C3Fp = Sl 2 sts to cn and hold in front of work, p1, k2 from cn

⬚ Cr5 = Sl 2 knit sts and 1 purl st to cn and hold in front of work, k2, sl the purl st on cn back to left needle and purl it; knit the last 2 sts on cn

# NO. 28  A DIAMOND WITH A KNOT

**QR codes: C6Bp, C6Fp, C12F**

Here's a diamond supported by cables. The repeat is 24 stitches and 40 rows and it's used on the Throw (see page 128).

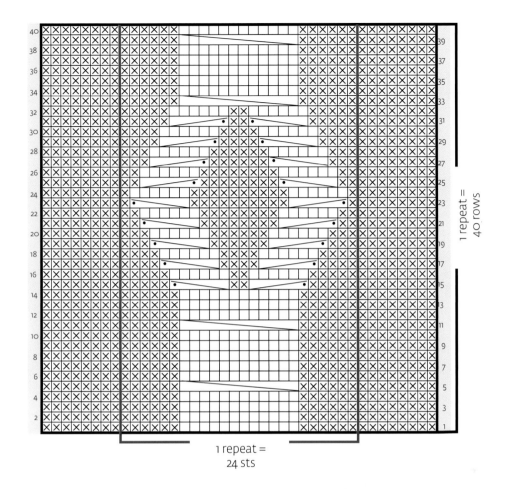

1 repeat =
40 rows

1 repeat =
24 sts

CO 40 sts.

**Rows 1 and 3:** P14, k12, p14.
**Rows 2 and 4:** K14, p12, k14.
**Row 5:** P14, C12F, p14.
**Rows 6-10:** Work as for Rows 2-3.
**Row 11:** P14, C12F, p14.
**Rows 12-14:** Work as for Rows 2-3.
**Row 15:** P13, C6Bp, p2, C6Fp, p13.
**Row 16:** K13, p6, k2, p6, k13.
**Row 17:** P12, C6Bp, p4, C6Fp, p12.
**Row 18:** K12, p6, k4, p6, k12.
**Row 19:** P11, C6Bp, p6, C6Fp, p11.
**Row 20:** K11, p6, k6, p6, k11.
**Row 21:** P10, C6Bp, p8, C6Fp, p10.
**Row 22:** K10, p6, k8, p6, k10.
**Row 23:** P9, C6Bp, p10, C6Fp, p9.
**Row 24:** K9, p6, k10, p6, k9.
**Row 25:** P10, C6Fp, p8, C6Bp, p10.
**Row 26:** K10, p6, k8, p6, k10.
**Row 27:** P11, C6Fp, p6, C6Bp, p11.
**Row 28:** K11, p6, k6, p6, k11.
**Row 29:** P12, C6Fp, p4, C6Bp, p12.
**Row 30:** K12, p6, k4, p6, k12.
**Row 31:** P13, C6Fp, p2, C6Bp, p13.
**Row 32:** K13, p6, k2, p6, k13.
**Row 33:** P14, C12F, p14.

**Row 34:** K14, p12, k14.
**Row 35:** P14, k12, p14.
**Row 36:** K14, p12, k14.
**Row 37:** P14, k12, p14.
**Row 38:** K14, p12, k14.
**Row 39:** P14, C12F, p14.
**Row 40:** K14, p12, k14.

☐   Knit on RS, purl on WS

☒   Purl on RS, knit on WS

C6Bp = Sl 1 purl st to cn and hold in back of work, k5, p1 from cn

C6Fp = Sl 5 knit sts to cn and hold in front of work, p1, k5 from cn

C12F = Sl 6 sts to cn and hold in front of work, k6, k6 from cn.

# NO. 29 A DIAMOND FILLED WITH SEED STITCH

**QR codes: C1/3R, C3/1L, C4Bp, C4Fp, C6F**

Here's a diamond filled with seed stitch and supported by cables. The repeat is 22 stitches and 40 rows.

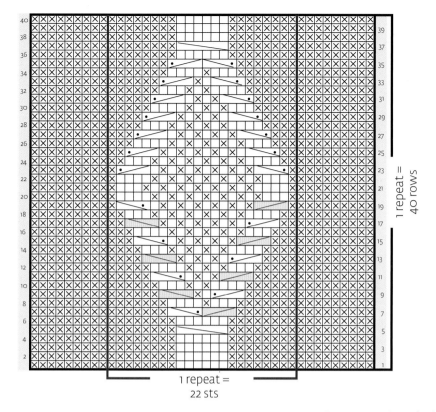

1 repeat =
40 rows

1 repeat =
22 sts

CO 40 sts.

**Rows 1 and 3:** P17, k6, p17.
**Rows 2 and 4:** K17, p6, k17.
**Row 5:** P17, C6F, p17.
**Row 6:** K17, p6, k17.
**Row 7:** P16, C1/3R, C4Fp, p16.
**Row 8:** K16, p4, k1, p3, k16.
**Row 9:** P15, C4Bp, k1, p1, C3/1L, p15.
**Row 10:** K15, p3, k1, p1, k1, p4, k15.
**Row 11:** P14, C1/3R, p1, k1, p1, k1, C4Fp, p14.
**Row 12:** K14, p4, k1, p1, k1, p1, k1, p3, k14.
**Row 13:** P13, C4Bp, (k1, p1) 3 times, C3/1L, p13.
**Row 14:** K13, p3, (k1, p1) 4 times, p3, k13.
**Row 15:** P12, C1/3R, (p1, k1) 4 times, C4Fp, p12.
**Row 16:** K12, p3, (p1, k1) 5 times, p3, k12.
**Row 17:** P11, C4Bp, (k1, p1) 5 times, C3/1L, p11.
**Row 18:** K11, p3, (k1, p1) 6 times, p3, k11.
**Row 19:** P10, C1/3R, (p1, k1) 6 times, C4Fp, p10.
**Row 20:** K10, p3, (p1, k1) 7 times, p3, k10.
**Row 21:** P10, k4, (p1, k1) 7 times, k2, p10.
**Row 22:** K10, p3, (p1, k1) 7 times, p3, k10.
**Row 23:** P10, C4Fp, (p1, k1) 6 times, C4Bp, p10.
**Row 24:** K11, p3, (k1, p1) 6 times, p3, k11.
**Row 25:** P11, C4Fp, (k1, p1) 5 times, C4Bp, p11.
**Row 26:** K12, p3, (p1, k1) 5 times, p3, k12.
**Row 27:** P12, C4Fp, (p1, k1) 4 times, C4Bp, p12.
**Row 28:** K13, p3, (k1, p1) 4 times, p3, k13.
**Row 29:** P13, C4Fp, (k1, p1) 3 times, C4Bp, p13.
**Row 30:** K14, p3, (k1, p1) 3 times, p3, k14.

**Row 31:** P14, C4Fp, (p1, k1) 2 times, C4Bp, p14.
**Row 32:** K15, p3, (k1, p1) 2 times, p3, k15.
**Row 33:** P15, C4Fp, k1, p1, C4Bp, p15.
**Row 34:** K16, p4, k1, p3, k16.
**Row 35:** P16, C4Fp, C4Bp, p16.
**Row 36:** K17, p6, k17.
**Row 37:** P17, C6F, p17.
**Row 38:** K17, p6, k17.
**Row 39:** P17, k6, p17.
**Row 40:** K17, p6, k17.

☐ Knit on RS, purl on WS

☒ Purl on RS, knit on WS

▱ C1/3R = Sl 1 st to cn and hold in back of work, k3, k1 from cn

▱ C4Bp = Sl 1 st to cn and hold in back of work, k3, p1 from cn

▱ C3/1L = Sl 3 sts to cn and hold in front of work, k1, k3 from cn

▱ C4Fp = Sl 3 sts to cn and hold in front of work, p1, k3 from cn

▱ C6F = Sl 3 sts to cn and hold in front of work, k3, k3 from cn

# Cables and Lace

Cables and lace combine for charming patterns and effects. It might seem a little discouraging to knit both lace and cable patterns at the same time, but once you've learned how to read the charts, you'll quickly understand the logic.

# NO. 30  WINGED CABLE

**QR codes: C6F and C6B**

The combination of cables and lace makes a charming effect. The pattern repeats over 24 stitches and 24 rows. As the chart shows, groups of 12 rows stagger so that you have cables over lace and lace over cables. The chart shows one-and-a-half repeats.

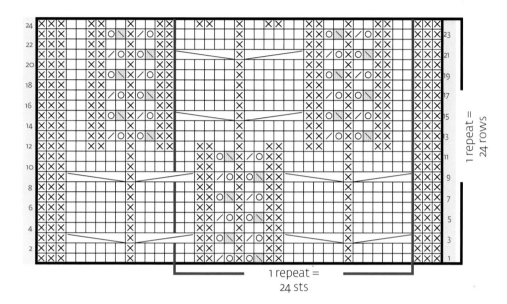

1 repeat = 24 rows

1 repeat = 24 sts

CO 41 sts.

**Row 1:** P3, k6, p1, k6, p2, k2tog tbl, yo, p1, yo, k2tog, p2, k6, p1, k6, p3.
**Rows 2, 4, 6, 8, and 10:** K3, p6, k1, p6, k2, p2, k1, p2, k2, p6, k1, p6, k3.
**Row 3:** P3, C6B, p1, C6F, p2, yo, k2tog, p1, k2tog tbl, yo, p2, C6B, p1, C6F, p3.
**Row 5:** P3, k6, p1, k6, p2, k2tog tbl, yo, p1, yo, k2tog, p2, k6, p1, k6, p3.
**Row 7:** P3, k6, p1, k6, p2, yo, k2tog, p1, k2tog tbl, yo, p2, k6, p1, k6, p3.
**Row 9:** P3, C6B, p1, C6F, p2, yo, k2tog tbl, p1, k2tog, yo, p2, C6B, p1, C6F, p3.
**Row 11:** P3, k6, p1, k6, p2, yo, k2tog, p1, k2tog tbl, yo, p2, k6, p1, k6, p3.
**Row 12:** K3, (p2, k2, p2, k1, p2, k2) 3 times, p2, k3.
**Row 13:** P3, k2, p2, k2tog tbl, yo, p1, yo, k2tog, p2, k6, p1, k6, p2, k2tog tbl, yo, p1, yo, k2tog, p2, k2, p3.
**Rows 14, 16, 18, 20, and 22:** K3, p2, k2, p2, k1, p2, k2, p6, k1, p6, k2, p2, k1, p2, k2, p2, k3.
**Row 15:** P3, k2, p2, yo, k2tog, p1, k2tog tbl, yo, p2, C6B, p1, C6F, p2, yo, k2tog, p1, k2tog tbl, yo, p2, k2, p3.

**Row 17:** P3, k2, p2, k2tog tbl, yo, p1, yo, k2tog, p2, k6, p1, k6, p2, k2tog tbl, yo, p1, yo, k2tog, p2, k2, p3.
**Row 19:** P3, k2, p2, yo, k2tog, p1, k2tog tbl, yo, p2, k6, p1, k6, p2, yo, k2tog, p1, k2tog tbl, yo, p2, k2, p3.
**Row 21:** P3, k2, p2, k2tog tbl, yo, p1, yo, k2tog, p2, C6B, p1, C6F, p2, k2tog tbl, yo, p1, yo, k2tog, p2, k2, p3.
**Row 23:** P3, k2, p2, yo, k2tog, p1, k2tog tbl, yo, p2, k6, p1, k6, p2, yo, k2tog, p1, k2tog tbl, yo, p2, k2, p3.
**Row 24:** Work as for Row 12.

Rep Rows 1–16 once more = 40 rows.

| | |
|---|---|
| ☐ | Knit on RS, purl on WS |
| ☒ | Purl on RS, knit on WS |
| ◺ | K2tog tbl |
| ◿ | K2tog |
| ◯ | Yo |
| ◻◹ | C6F = Sl 3 sts to cn and hold in front of work, k3, k3 from cn |
| ◻◸ | C4B = Sl 3 sts to cn and hold in back of work, k3, k3 from cn |

# NO. 31  LEAF CABLES

---

**QR codes: C4pF**
This motif features a little cable with a leaf pattern on each side of the cable. The repeat is worked over 12 stitches and 5 rows. The chart shows 3 repeats across and 2 up. The leaf cable pattern is used on Maj's Ankle Socks (see page 146).

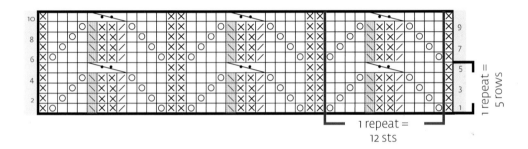

1 repeat = 12 sts

1 repeat = 5 rows

CO 42 sts.

**Row 1:** P1, (yo, k3, k2tog, p2, k2tog tbl, k3, yo, p2) 2 times, yo, k3, k2tog, p2, k2tog tbl, k3, yo, p1.
**Row 2:** K1, (p1, yo, p2, p2tog tbl, k2, p2tog, p2, yo, p1, k2) 2 times, p1, yo, p2, p2tog tbl, k2, p2tog, p2, yo, p1, k1.
**Row 3:** P1, (k2, yo, k1, k2tog, p2, k2tog tbl, k1, yo, k2, p2) 2 times, k2, yo, k1, k2tog, p2, k2tog tbl, k1, yo, k2, p1.
**Row 4:** K1, (p3, yo, p2tog tbl, k2, p2tog, yo, p3, k2) 2 times, p3, yo, p2tog tbl, k2, p2tog, yo, p3, k1.
**Row 5:** P1, (k4, C4pF, k4, p2) 2 times, k4, C4pF, k4, p1.
**Row 6:** K1, (yo, p3, p2tog tbl, k2, p2tog, p3, yo, k2) 2 times, yo, p3, p2tog tbl, k2, p2tog, p3, yo, k1.
**Row 7:** P1, (k1, yo, k2, k2tog, p2, k2tog tbl, k2, yo, k1, p2) 2 times, k1, yo, k2, k2tog, p2, k2tog tbl, k2, yo, k1, p1.
**Row 8:** K1, (p2, yo, p1, p2tog tbl, k2, p2tog, p1, yo, p2, k2) 2 times, p2, yo, p1, p2tog tbl, k2, p2tog, p1, yo, p2, k1.

**Row 9:** P1, (k3, yo, k2tog, p2, k2tog tbl, yo, k3, p2) 2 times, k3, yo, k2tog, p2, k2tog tbl, yo, k3, p1.
**Row 10:** K1, (p4, C4pF, p4, k2) 2 times, p4, C4pF, p4, k1.

Rep Rows 1-10 3 more times = 40 rows.

☐  Knit on RS, purl on WS

☒  Purl on RS, knit on WS

⊡  Yo

☑  K2tog on RS and p2tog on WS

◩  K2tog tbl on RS and p2tog tbl on WS

⬭  C4pF = *On RS:* Sl 1 knit st and 2 purl sts to cn and hold in front of work, k1, sl the two purl sts back to left needle and purl them, k1 from cn
*On WS:* Sl 1 purl st and 2 knit sts to cn and hold in front of work, p1, sl the 2 knit sts back on left needle and knit them, p1 from cn

# NO. 32  LACE CABLE

**QR codes: C6F and C6B**

This lace and cable motif waves back and forth. The repeat is worked over 6 stitches and 28 rows. The chart shows 4 repeats across and 1 up. The leaf cables surround the Glass Cozies on page 118.

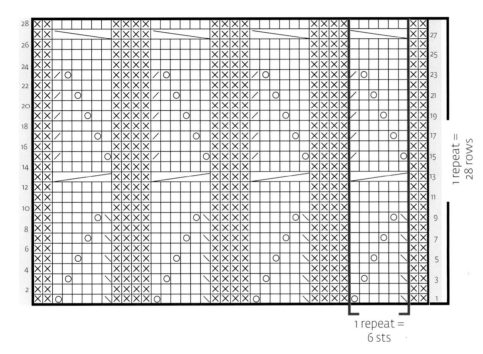

1 repeat = 28 rows

1 repeat = 6 sts

CO 40 sts.

**Row 1:** P2, (ssk, k4, yo, p4) 3 times, ssk, k4, yo, p2.
**Row 2 and all WS rows:** K2, (p6, k4) 3 times, p6, k2.
**Row 3:** P2, (ssk, k3, yo, k1, p4) 3 times, ssk, k3, yo, k1, p2.
**Row 5:** P2, (ssk, k2, yo, k2, p4) 3 times, ssk, k2, yo, k2, p2.
**Row 7:** P2, (ssk, k1, yo, k3, p4) 3 times, ssk, k1, yo, k3, p2.
**Row 9:** P2, (ssk, yo, k4, p4) 3 times, ssk, yo, k4, p2.
**Row 11:** P2, (k6, p4) 3 times, k6, p2.
**Row 13:** P2, (C6B, p4) 3 times, C6B, p2.
**Row 15:** P2, (yo, k4, k2tog, p4) 3 times, yo, k4, k2tog, p2.
**Row 17:** P2, (k1, yo, k3, k2tog, p4) 3 times, k1, yo, k3, k2tog, p2.
**Row 19:** P2, (k2, yo, k2, k2tog, p4) 3 times, k2, yo, k2, k2tog, p2.

**Row 21:** P2, (k3, yo, k1, k2tog, p4) 3 times, k3, yo, k1, k2tog, p2.
**Row 23:** P2, (k4, yo, k2tog, p4) 3 times, k4, yo, k2tog, p2.
**Row 25:** P2, (k6, p4) 3 times, k6, p2.
**Row 27:** P2, (C6F, p4) 3 times, C6F, p2.
**Row 28:** K2, (p6, k4) 3 times, p6, k2.

Now work Rows 1–12 once more = 40 rows.

☐  Knit on RS, purl on WS

☒  Purl on RS, knit on WS

◩  Ssk = (Sl 1 knitwise) 2 times and knit the 2 sts tog tbl or work as sl 1, k1, psso

◪  K2tog

◉  Yo

▱  C6B = Sl 3 sts to cn and hold in back of work, k3, k3 from cn

▱  C6F = Sl 3 sts to cn and hold in front of work, k3, k3 from cn

# NO. 33 SLITHERY CABLE

**QR codes: C4F, C4B, C4F2p, C4B2p**

The swatch shows two cables, one leaning to the right and the other to the left. The cables can be used together or separately. The cable repeats over 10 stitches and 8 rows.

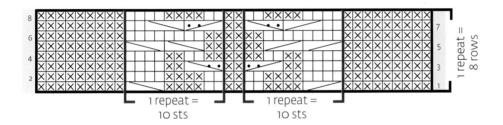

CO 40 sts.

**Row 1:** P9, C4B, p4, k2, p2, k2, p4, C4F, p9.
**Row 2:** K9, p4, k4, p2, k2, p2, k4, p4, k9.
**Row 3:** P9, k4, p2, C4B2p, p2, C4F2p, p2, k4, p9.
**Row 4:** K9, p4, k2, p2, k6, p2, k2, p4, k9.
**Row 5:** P9, (C4B) 2 times, p6, (C4F) 2 times, p9.
**Row 6:** K9, p8, k6, p8, k9.
**Row 7:** P9, k2, C4B, C4F2p, p2, C4B2p, C4F, k2, p9.
**Row 8:** K9, p4, k4, p2, k2, p2, k4, p4, k9.

Rep Rows 1-8 4 more times = 40 rows.

□ Knit on RS, purl on WS

☒ Purl on RS, knit on WS

C4F = Sl 2 sts to cn and hold in front of work, k2, k2 from cn

C4B = Sl 2 sts to cn and hold in back of work, k2, k2 from cn

C4F2p = Sl 2 sts to cn and hold in front of work, p2, k2 from cn

C4B2p = Sl 2 sts to cn and hold in back of work, p2, k2 from cn

# Celtic Cables

Celtic cables are those we connect with Aran patterns—cables that bend to the right and left to create fantastic patterns. These cable designs require concentration to master, but the resulting design is a reward worth striving for.

# NO. 34 LATTICE CABLE

**QR codes: C4B, C4B2p, and C4F2p**

This pattern features cable repeats that twist around each other on a reverse stockinette background. The chart shows repeats with 32 stitches and 16 rows. The cable appears on Sigrid's Poncho (see page 150).

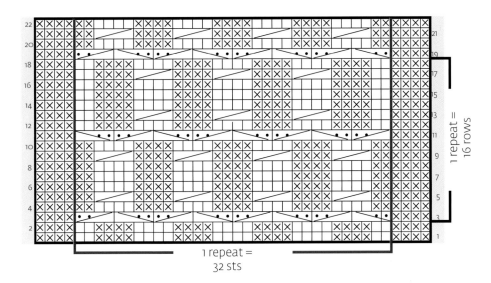

1 repeat = 16 rows

1 repeat = 32 sts

CO 40 sts.

**Row 1:** P4, k2, p4, (k4, p4) 3 times, k2, p4.
**Row 2:** K4, p2, k4, (p4, k4) 3 times, p2, k4.
**Row 3:** P4, (C4F2p, C4B2p) 4 times, p4.
**Row 4:** K6, p4, (k4, p4) 3 times, k6.
**Row 5:** P6, C4B, (p4, C4B) 3 times, p6.
**Row 6:** Work as for Row 4.
**Row 7:** P6, k4, (p4, k4) 3 times, p6.
**Row 8:** Work as for Row 4.
**Row 9:** Work as for Row 5.
**Row 10:** Work as for Row 4.
**Row 11:** P4, (C4B2p, C4F2p) 4 times, p4.
**Row 12:** K4, p2, k4, (p4, k4) 3 times, p2, k4.
**Row 13:** P4, k2, p4, (C4B, p4) 3 times, k2, p4.
**Row 14:** Work as for Row 12.
**Row 15:** P4, k2, p4, (k4, p4) 3 times, k2, p4.
**Row 16:** Work as for Row 12.
**Row 17:** Work as for Row 13.
**Row 18:** Work as for Row 12.

Rep Rows 3-18 once more.

**Row 19:** P4, (C4F2p, C4B2p) 4 times, p4.
**Row 20:** K6, p4, (k4, p4) 3 times, k6.
**Row 21:** P6, C4B, (p4, C4B) 3 times, p6.
**Row 22:** Work as for Row 20.

☐ Knit on RS, purl on WS

☒ Purl on RS, knit on WS

C4B = Sl 2 sts to cn and hold in back of work, k2, k2 from cn

C4B2p = Sl 2 sts to cn and hold in back of work, p2, k2 from cn

C4F2p = Sl 2 sts to cn and hold in front of work, k2, p2 from cn

# NO. 35 HEART CABLE

**QQR codes: C3Fp, C3Bp, C4F, C4B, C4F2p, and C4B2p**
This swatch shows the heart cable with the pattern repeated twice.
The cable repeats with 26 stitches and 20 rows. The cable appears on the Tunic with Heart Cables (see page 156).

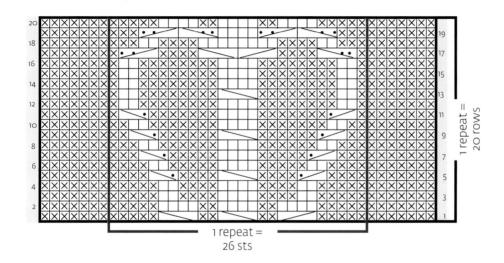

1 repeat = 26 sts

1 repeat = 20 rows

CO 40 sts.

**Row 1:** P12, C4B, p2, C4F, p2, C4F, p12.
**Row 2:** K12, p4, k2, p4, k2, p4, k12.
**Row 3:** P12, k2, p4, k4, p4, k2, p12.
**Row 4:** K12, p2, k4, p4, k4, p2, k12.
**Row 5:** P11, C3Bp, p4, C4F, p4, C3Fp, p11.
**Row 6:** K11, p2, k5, p4, k5, p2, k11.
**Row 7:** P10, C3Bp, p5, k4, p5, C3Fp, p10.
**Row 8:** K10, p2, k6, p4, k6, p2, k10.
**Row 9:** P9, C3Bp, p6, C4F, p6, C3Fp, p9.
**Row 10:** K9, p2, k7, p4, k7, p2, k9.
**Row 11:** P8, C3Bp, p7, k4, p7, C3Fp, p8.
**Row 12:** K8, p2, k8, p4, k8, p2, k8.
**Row 13:** P8, k2, p8, C4F, p8, k2, p8.
**Row 14:** K8, p2, k8, p4, k8, p2, k8.
**Row 15:** P8, k2, p8, k4, p8, k2, p8.
**Row 16:** K8, p2, k8, p4, k8, p2, k8.
**Row 17:** P8, C4F2p, p4, C4B, C4F, p4, C4B2p, p8.
**Row 18:** K10, p2, k4, p8, k4, p2, k10.
**Row 19:** P10, C4F2p, C4B2p, k4, C4F2p, C4B2p, p10.
**Row 20:** K12, p4, k2, p4, k2, p4, k12.

Rep Rows 1–20 once more = 40 rows.

| | Knit on RS, purl on WS |
|---|---|
| ☒ | Purl on RS, knit on WS |
| | C3Fp = Sl 2 sts to cn and hold in front of work, p1, k2 from cn |
| | C3Bp = Sl 1 st to cn and hold in back of work, k2, p1 from cn |
| | C4F = Sl 2 sts to cn and hold in front of work, k2, k2 from cn |
| | C4B = Sl 2 sts to cn and hold in back of work, k2, k2 from cn |
| | C4F2p = Sl 2 knit sts to cn and hold in front of work, p2, k2 from cn |
| | C4B2p = Sl 2 purl sts to cn and hold in back of work, k2, p2 from cn |

# NO. 36 OVER AND UNDER CABLE

**QR codes: C6pF andC6pB**

This swatch has a cable repeated twice up. The repeat is worked over 14 stitches and 20 rows. It's used on the Men's Aran Sweater (see page 162).

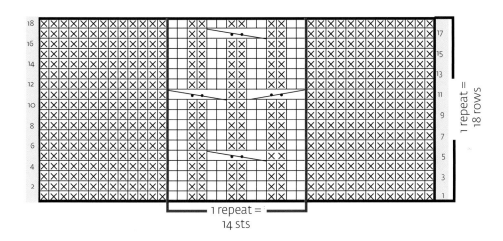

CO 40 sts.

**Row 1:** P13, (k2, p2) 3 times, k2, p13.
**Row 2 and all WS rows:** K13, (p2, k2) 3 times, p2, k13.
**Row 3:** Work as for Row 1.
**Row 5:** P13, k2, p2, C6pF, p2, k2, p13.
**Rows 7 and 9:** Work as for Row 1.
**Row 11:** P13, C6pB, p2, C6pF, p13.
**Rows 13 and 15:** Work as for Row 1.
**Row 17:** Work as for Row 5.
**Row 18:** K13, (p2, k2) 3 times, p2, k13.

Rep Rows 1-18 once more and then work Rows 1-4 = 40 rows.

☐ Knit on RS, purl on WS

☒ Purl on RS, knit on WS

C6pF = Sl 2 knit and 2 purl sts to cn and hold in front of work, k2, sl the 2 purl sts to left needle and purl them, k2 from cn

C6pB = Sl 2 knit and 2 purl sts to cn and hold in back of work, k2, sl the 2 purl sts back on left needle and purl them, k2 from cn

# NO. 37 CELTIC KNOT

**QR codes: C4Fp, C4Bp, C6F, andC6B**
The chart shows one cable repeat over 28 stitches and 40 rows. The Celtic Knot embellishes Ingeborg's Hat on page 154.

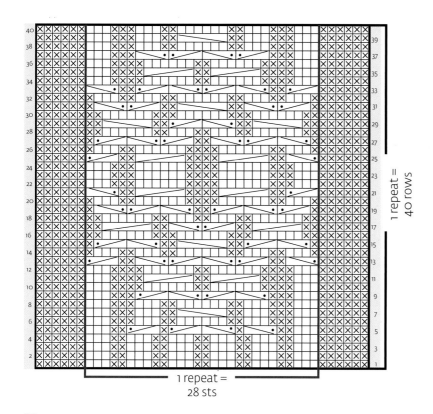

**1 repeat = 40 rows**

**1 repeat = 28 sts**

CO 40 sts.

**Rows 1 and 3:** P6, (k3, p2) 5 times, k3, p6.
**Rows 2 and 4:** K6, (p3, k2) 5 times, p3, k6.
**Row 5:** P6, k3, p2, C4Fp, p1, C4Fp, C4Bp, p1, C4Bp, p2, k3, p6.
**Row 6:** K6, p3, k3, p3, k2, p6, k2, p3, k3, p3, k6.
**Row 7:** P6, k3, p3, k3, p2, C6F, p2, k3, p3, k3, p6.
**Row 8:** K6, p3, k3, p3, k2, p6, k2, p3, k3, p3, k6.
**Row 9:** P6, k3, p3, (C4Fp, C4Bp) 2 times, p3, k3, p6.
**Row 10:** K6, p3, k4, p6, k2, p6, k4, p3, k6.
**Row 11:** P6, k3, p4, C6B, p2, C6B, p4, k3, p6.
**Row 12:** K6, p3, k4, p6, k2, p6, k4, p3, k6.
**Row 13:** P6, C4Fp, p2, (C4Bp, C4Fp) 2 times, p2, C4B, p6.
**Row 14:** K7, p3, k2, p3, k2, p6, k2, p3, k2, p3, k7.
**Row 15:** P7, C4Fp, C4Bp, p2, C6F, p2, C4Fp, C4Bp, p7.
**Row 16:** K8, p6, k3, p6, k3, p6, k8.
**Row 17:** P8, C6B, p2, C4Bp, C4Fp, p2, C6B, p8.
**Row 18:** K8, p6, k2, p3, k2, p3, k2, p6, k8.
**Row 19:** P7, C4Bp, C4Fp, C4Bp, p2, C4Fp, C4Bp, C4Fp, p7.
**Row 20:** K7, p3, k2, p6, k4, p6, k2, p3, k7.
**Row 21:** P6, C4Bp, p2, C6B, p4, C6B, p2, C4Fp, p6.
**Row 22:** K6, p3, k3, p6, k4, p6, k3, p3, k6.
**Row 23:** P6, k3, p3, k6, p4, k6, p3, k3, p6.
**Row 24:** K6, p3, k3, p6, k4, p6, k3, p3, k6.

**Row 25:** P6, C4Fp, p2, C6B, p4, C6B, p2, C4Bp, p6.
**Row 26:** K7, p3, k2, p6, k4, p6, k2, p3, k7.
**Row 27:** P7, C4Fp, C4Bp, C4Fp, p2, C4Bp, C4Fp, C4Bp, p7.
**Row 28:** K8, p6, k2, p3, k2, p3, k2, p6, k8.
**Row 29:** P8, C6F, p2, C4Fp, C4Bp, p2, C6F, p8.
**Row 30:** K8, p6, k3, p6, k3, p6, k8.
**Row 31:** P7, C4Bp, C4Fp, p2, C6F, p2, C4Bp, C4Fp, p7.
**Row 32:** K7, p3, k2, p3, k2, p6, k2, p3, k2, p3, k7.
**Row 33:** P6, C4Bp, p2, (C4Fp, C4Bp) 2 times, p2, C4Fp, p6.
**Row 34:** K6, p3, k4, p6, k2, p6, k4, p3, k6.
**Row 35:** P6, k3, p4, C6B, p2, C6B, p4, k3, p6.
**Row 36:** K6, p3, k4, p6, k2, p6, k4, p3, k6.
**Row 37:** P6, k3, p3, (C4Bp, C4Fp) 2 times, p3, k3, p6.
**Row 38:** K6, p3, k3, p3, k2, p6, k2, p3, k3, p3, k6.
**Row 39:** P6, k3, p3, k3, p2, C6F, p2, k3, p3, k3, p6.
**Row 40:** K6, p3, k3, p3, k2, p6, k2, p3, k3, p3, k6.

☐ Knit on RS, purl on WS

☒ Purl on RS, knit on WS

C4Fp = Sl 3 sts to cn and hold in front of work, p1, k3 from cn

C4Bp = Sl 1 st to cn and hold in back of work, k3, p1 from cn

C6F = Sl 3 sts to cn and hold in front of work, k3, k3 from cn

C6B = Sl 3 sts to cn and hold in back of work, k3, k3 from cn

# Cables with Twisted Knit Stitches

Working cables with twisted knit stitches in combination with purl stitches creates pretty patterns, but the technique can be challenging if you work back and forth. The twisted stitches must also be twisted on the wrong side by working purls through the back loops.

# NO. 38 SEAGRASS

**QR codes: Tw2L, Tw2R, C2BTw Rib, C2FTw Rib, and C3FTw Rib**

This cable is worked with twisted knit stitches on the right side and twisted purls on the wrong side. Some knitters think this technique is somewhat difficult, but, with practice, it can become just as quick as working regular purl stitches. The repeat is worked over 27 stitches and 16 rows. You can see the pattern on the Bolero on page 165.

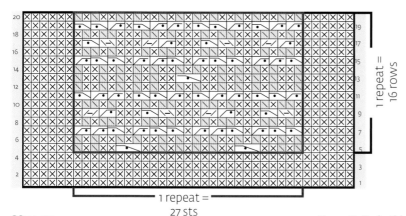

1 repeat = 27 sts

1 repeat = 16 rows

CO 39 sts.

**Rows 1 and 3:** P39.
**Rows 2 and 4:** K39.
**Row 5:** P6, k1tbl, p1, k1tbl, p2, C3FTw Rib, p2, (k1tbl, p1) 3 times, k1tbl, p2, C3FTw Rib, p2, k1tbl, p1, k1tbl, p6.
**Row 6:** K6, (p1tbl, k1, p1tbl, k2) 2 times, (p1tbl, k1) 3 times, p1tbl, (k2, p1tbl, k1, p1tbl) 2 times, k6.
**Row 7:** P6, (C2FTw Rib) 2 times, C2BTw Rib, p1, C2FTw Rib, (C2BTw Rib) 2 times, p1, (C2FTw Rib) 2 times, C2BTw Rib, p1, C2FTw Rib, (C2FTw Rib) 2 times, p6.
**Row 8:** K7, p1tbl, k1, p2tbl, k3, p2tbl, k1, p1tbl, k3, p1tbl, k1, p2tbl, k3, p2tbl, k1, p1tbl, k7.
**Row 9:** P7, Tw2L, C2FTw Rib, p3, C2BTw Rib, Tw2R, k3, Tw2L, C2FTw Rib, p3, C2BTw Rib, Tw2R, p7.
**Row 10:** K7, p2tbl, k1, p1tbl, k3, p1tbl, k1, p2tbl, k3, p2tbl, k1, p1tbl, k3, p1tbl, k1, p2tbl, k7.
**Row 11:** P6, C2BTw Rib, (C2FTw Rib) 2 times, p1, (C2BTw Rib) 2 times, C2FTw Rib, p1, C2BTw Rib, (C2FTw Rib) 2 times, p1, (C2BTw Rib) 2 times, C2FTw Rib, p6.
**Row 12:** K6, p1tbl, k2, (p1tbl, k1) 3 times, p1tbl, k2, p1tbl, k1, p1tbl, k2, (p1tbl, k1) 3 times, p1tbl, k2, p1tbl, k6.
**Row 13:** P6, k1tbl, p2, (k1tbl, p1) 3 times, k1tbl, p2, C3FTw Rib, p2, (k1tbl, p1) 3 times, k1tbl, p2, k1tbl, p6.
**Row 14:** Work as for Row 12.
**Row 15:** P6, C2FTw Rib, (C2BTw Rib) 2 times, p1, (C2FTw Rib) 2 times, C2BTw Rib, p1, C2FTw Rib, (C2FTw Rib) 2 times, p1, (C2FTw Rib) 2 times, C2BTw Rib, p6.

**Row 16:** K7, (p1tbl, k1, p2tbl, k3) 3 times, p1tbl, k1, p2tbl, k7.
**Row 17:** P7, C2BTw Rib, Tw2R, p3, Tw2L, C2FTw Rib, p3, C2BTw Rib, Tw2R, p3, Tw2L, C2FTw Rib, p7.
**Row 18:** K7, p1tbl, k1, p2tbl, k3, p2tbl, k1, p1tbl, k3, p1tbl, k1, p2tbl, k3, p2tbl, k1, p1tbl, k7.
**Row 19:** P6, (C2BTw Rib) 2 times, C2FTw Rib, p1, C2BTw Rib, (C2FTw Rib) 2 times, p1, (C2BTw Rib) 2 times, C2FTw Rib, p1, C2BTw Rib, (C2FTw Rib) 2 times, p6.
**Row 20:** K6, (p1tbl, k1, p1tbl, k2) 2 times, (p1tbl, k1) 3 times, p1tbl, (k2, p1tbl, k1, p1tbl) 2 times, k6.

Rep Rows 5-20 once more and end with Rows 1-4 = 40 rows.

☒  Purl on RS, knit on WS

◻  Twisted knit on RS, twisted purl on WS

⬓  Tw2L = Sl 1 st to cn and hold in front of work, k1tbl, k1tbl from cn

⬔  Tw2R - Sl 1 st to cn and hold in back of work, k1tbl, k1tbl from cn

⬓  C2BTw Rib = Sl 1 st to cn and hold in back of work, k1tbl, p1 from cn

⬔  C2FTw Rib = Sl 1 st to cn and hold in front of work, p1, k1tbl from cn

⬓  C3FTw Rib = Sl 2 sts to cn and hold in front of work, k1tbl, sl 1 st back on left needle and p1, k1tbl from cn

# NO. 39 CIRCULAR CABLE

**QR codes: C2BTw Rib, C2FTw Rib, and C7FTw Rib**
This swatch consists of three identical repeats of circular cables worked with twisted stitches. The cable repeats over 11 stitches and 12 rows.

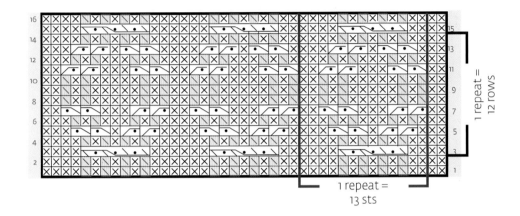

1 repeat = 12 rows

1 repeat = 13 sts

CO 41 sts.

**Row 1:** P4, (k1tbl, p1) 3 times, k1tbl, p6, (k1tbl, p1) 3 times, k1tbl, p6, (k1tbl, p1) 3 times, k1tbl, p4.
**Row 2:** K4, (p1tbl, k1) 3 times, p1tbl, k6, (p1tbl, k1) 3 times, p1tbl, k6, (p1tbl, k1) 3 times, p1tbl, k4.
**Row 3:** P4, (C7FTw Rib, p6) 2 times, C7FTw Rib, p4.
**Row 4:** Work as for Row 2.
**Row 5:** P3, *(C2BTw Rib) 2 times, p1, (C2FTw Rib) 2 times, p4*. Rep * to * once more and end with (C2BTw Rib) 2 times, p1, (C2FTw Rib) 2 times, p3.
**Row 6:** K3, (p1tbl, k1, p1tbl, k3, p1tbl, k1, p1tbl, k4) 2 times, p1tbl, k1, p1tbl, k3, p1tbl, k1, p1tbl, k3.
**Row 7:** P2, *(C2BTw Rib) 2 times, p3, (C2FTw Rib) 2 times, p2*. Rep * to * two more times.
**Row 8:** K2, p1tbl, k1, p1tbl, (k5, p1tbl, k1, p1tbl, k2, p1tbl, k1, p1tbl) 2 times, k5, p1tbl, k1, p1tbl, k2.
**Row 9:** P2, k1tbl, p1, k1tbl, (p5, k1tbl, p1, k1tbl, p2, k1tbl, p1, k1tbl) 2 times, p5, k1tbl, p1, k1tbl, p2.
**Row 10:** Work as for Row 8.
**Row 11:** *P2, (C2FTw Rib) 2 times, p3, (C2BTw Rib) 2 times*. Rep * to * 3 more times and end with p2.

**Row 12:** K3, (p1tbl, k1, p1tbl, k3, p1tbl, k1, p1tbl, k4) 2 times, p1tbl, k1, p1tbl, k3, p1tbl, k1, p1tbl, k3.
**Row 13:** P3, *(C2FTw Rib) 2 times, p1, (C2BTw Rib) 2 times, p4*. Rep * to * once more and end with (C2FTw Rib) 2 times, p1, (C2BTw Rib) 2 times, p3.
**Row 14:** K4, (p1tbl, k1) 3 times, p1tbl, k6, (p1tbl, k1) 3 times, p1tbl, k6, (p1tbl, k1) 3 times, p1tbl, k4.

Rep Rows 3–14 twice more.

**Row 15:** P4, (C7FTw Rib, p6) 2 times, C7FTw Rib, p4.
**Row 16:** K4, (p1tbl, k1) 3 times, p1tbl, k6, (p1tbl, k1) 3 times, p1tbl, k6, (p1tbl, k1) 3 times, p1tbl, k4.

| | |
|---|---|
| ◩ | Twisted knit on RS, twisted purl on WS |
| ☒ | Purl on RS, knit on WS |
| ◩ | C2BTw Rib = Sl 1 st to cn and hold in back of work, k1tbl, p1 from cn |
| ◩ | C2FTw Rib = Sl 1 st to cn and hold in front of work, p1, k1tbl from cn |
| ◩ | C7F Tw Rib = Sl 3 sts to cn and hold in front of work, k1tbl, p1, k1tbl, p1; from cn, work k1tbl, p1, k1tbl |

# NO. 40 TWISTED RIB CABLE

**QR code: C7FTw Rib**

This swatch shows four identical repeats of twisted rib stitches. The cable repeats over 7 stitches and 8 rows. You'll find this cable pattern on the Bolero (see page 165).

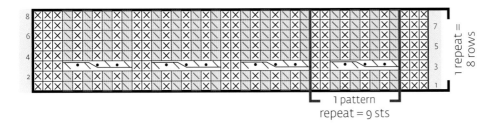

1 repeat = 8 rows

1 pattern repeat = 9 sts

CO 40 sts.

**Row 1:** P3, *(k1tbl, p1) 3 times, k1tbl, p2*. Rep * to * 2 more times and end with (k1tbl, p1) 3 times, k1tbl, p3.
**Row 2 and all WS rows:** K3, *(p1tbl, k1) 3 times, p1tbl, k2*. Rep * to * 2 more times and end with (p1tbl, k1) 3 times, p1tbl, k3.
**Row 3:** P3, (C7FTw Rib, p2) 3 times, C7FTw Rib, p3.
**Rows 5 and 7:** Work as for Row 1.
**Row 8:** K3, *(p1tbl, k1) 3 times, p1tbl, k2*. Rep * to * 2 more times and end with (p1tbl, k1) 3 times, p1tbl, k3.

Rep Rows 1-8 4 more times = 40 rows.

☐ Twisted knit on RS, twisted purl on WS

☒ Purl on RS, knit on WS

C7FTw Rib = Sl 3 sts to cn and hold in front of work, k1tbl, p1, k1tbl, p1; from cn, p1, k1tbl, p1, k1tbl

## Wrapped Stitches

Here's an unbelievably fun way to knit cables. Actually, these aren't technically cables, since the stitches don't change places. Instead, you place a small number of stitches on a cable needle so you can wrap the yarn clockwise twice around them, and then you slip those same stitches to the right needle without knitting them. Add twisted stitches and you have quite a decorative pattern.

# NO. 41 DOUBLE-WRAPPED CABLE

**QR code: Wr4**

The three identical cables on this swatch have a pattern repeat of 10 stitches and 8 rows. The motif is featured on the Celtic-Inspired Sweater (see page 170).

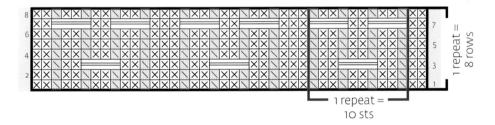

1 repeat = 8 rows

1 repeat = 10 sts

CO 40 sts.

**Row 1:** (P2, k1tbl) 4 times, p3, (k1tbl, p2) 3 times, k1tbl, p3, (k1tbl, p2) 4 times.
**Row 2:** (K2, p1tbl) 4 times, k3, (p1tbl, k2) 3 times, p1tbl, k3, (p1tbl, k2) 4 times.
**Row 3:** P2, k1tbl, p2, (Wr4, p2, k1tbl, p3, k1tbl, p2) 2 times, Wr4, p2, k1tbl, p2.
**Row 4:** Work as for Row 2.
**Row 5:** Work as for Row 1.
**Row 6:** Work as for Row 2.
**Row 7:** P2, (Wr4, p2, Wr4, p3) 2 times, (Wr4, p2) 2 times.
**Row 8:** Work as for Row 2.

Rep Rows 1-8 4 more times = 40 rows.

 Twisted knit on RS, twisted purl on WS

☒ Purl on RS, knit on WS

══ Wr4 = Sl 4 sts to cn and hold in front of work, wrap the yarn clockwise twice around the stitches and then sl the 4 sts to the right needle without knitting them

# NO. 42  SHOAL OF HERRINGS

**QR code: Wr3**

This swatch shows two identical patterns, each with a repeat of 17 stitches and 40 rows. The motif is featured on the Celtic-Inspired Sweater (see page 170).

CO 40 sts.

**Row 1 (RS):** P10, k1tbl, p1, k1tbl, p14, k1tbl, p1, k1tbl, p10.

**Row 2:** K10, p1tbl, k1, p1tbl, k14, p1tbl, k1, p1tbl, k10.

**Row 3:** P8, (k1tbl, p1) 3 times, k1tbl, p10, (k1tbl, p1) 3 times, k1tbl, p8.

**Row 4:** K8, (p1tbl, k1) 3 times, p1tbl, k10, (p1tbl, k1) 3 times, p1tbl, k8.

**Row 5:** P6, (k1tbl, p1) 5 times, k1tbl, p6, (k1tbl, p1) 5 times, k1tbl, p6.

**Row 6:** K6, (p1tbl, k1) 5 times, p1tbl, k6, (p1tbl, k1) 5 times, p1tbl, k6.

**Row 7:** P4, (k1tbl, p1) 7 times, k1tbl, p2, (k1tbl, p1) 7 times, k1tbl, p4.

**Row 8:** K4, (p1tbl, k1) 7 times, p1tbl, k2, (p1tbl, k1) 7 times, p1tbl, k4.

**Rows 9-14:** Rep Rows 7-8 3 times.

**Row 15:** P4, (k1tbl, p1) 3 times, Wr3, (p1, k1tbl) 3 times, p2, (k1tbl, p1) 3 times, Wr3, (p1, k1tbl) 3 times, p4.

**Row 16:** K4, (p1tbl, k1) 7 times, p1tbl, k2, (p1tbl, k1) 7 times, p1tbl, k4.

**Row 17:** P4, (k1tbl, p1) 2 times, Wr3, p1, Wr3, (p1, k1tbl) 2 times, p2, (k1tbl, p1) 2 times, Wr3, p1, Wr3, (p1, k1tbl) 2 times, p4.

**Row 18:** Work as for Row 16.

**Row 19:** P4, k1tbl, p1, (Wr3, p1) 3 times, k1tbl, p2, k1tbl, p1, (Wr3, p1) 3 times, k1tbl, p4.

**Row 20:** Work as for Row 16.

**Row 21:** P4, (Wr3, p1) 3 times, Wr3, p2, (Wr3, p1) 3 times, Wr3, p4.

**Row 22:** Work as for Row 16.

**Row 23:** P4, k1tbl, p1, (Wr3, p1) 3 times, k1tbl, p2, k1tbl, p1, (Wr3, p1) 3 times, k1tbl, p4.

**Row 24:** K4, (p1tbl, k1) 7 times, p1tbl, k2, (p1tbl, k1) 7 times, p1tbl, k4.

**Row 25:** P4, (k1tbl, p1) 2 times, Wr3, p1, Wr3, (p1, k1tbl) 2 times, p2, (k1tbl, p1) 2 times, Wr3, p1, Wr3, (p1, k1tbl) 2 times, p4.

**Row 26:** Work as for Row 24.

**Row 27:** P4, (k1tbl, p1) 3 times, Wr3, (p1, k1tbl) 3 times, p2, (k1tbl, p1) 3 times, Wr3, (p1, k1tbl) 3 times, p4.

**Row 28:** Work as for Row 24.

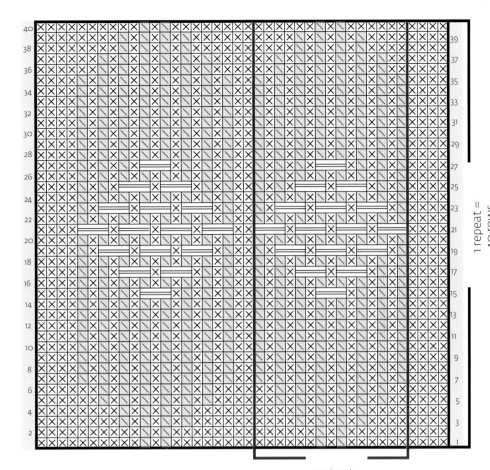

1 repeat = 40 rows

1 repeat = 15 sts

**Row 29:** P4, (k1tbl, p1) 7 times, k1tbl, p2, (k1tbl, p1) 7 times, k1tbl, p4.

**Row 30:** K4, (p1tbl, k1) 7 times, p1tbl, k2, (p1tbl, k1) 7 times, p1tbl, k4.

**Rows 31-35:** Rep Rows 29-30 2 times and then rep Row 29.

**Row 36 (WS):** K6, (p1tbl, k1) 5 times, p1tbl, k6, (p1tbl, k1) 5 times, p1tbl, k6.

**Row 37:** P6, (k1tbl, p1) 5 times, k1tbl, p6, (k1tbl, p1) 5 times, k1tbl, p6.

**Row 38:** K8, (p1tbl, k1) 3 times, p1tbl, k10, (p1tbl, k1) 3 times, p1tbl, k8.

**Row 39:** P8, (k1tbl, p1) 3 times, k1tbl, p10, (k1tbl, p1) 3 times, k1tbl, p8.

**Row 40:** K10, p1tbl, k1, p1tbl, k14, p1tbl, k1, p1tbl, k10.

☑ Twisted knit on RS, twisted purl on WS

☒ Purl on RS, knit on WS

▤ Wr3 = Sl 3 sts to cn and hold in front of work, wrap the yarn clockwise twice around the stitches and then sl the 3 sts to the right needle without knitting them

# NO. 43 CELTIC INSPIRATION

**QR code: Wr4**

This cable pattern has a repeat of 22 stitches and 40 rows. If you want to use the motif with continuous repeats, just work the first 28 stitches in the pattern and then repeat them. This cable is featured on the Celtic-Inspired Sweater (see page 170).

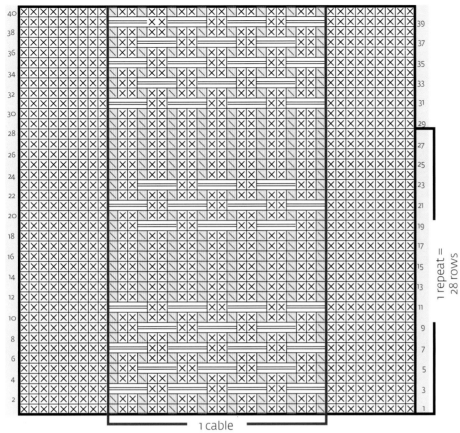

1 repeat = 28 rows

1 cable
repeat = 22 sts

CO 40 sts.

**Row 1 (RS):** P9, (k1tbl, p2) 7 times, k1tbl, p9.
**Row 2 and all WS rows:** K9, (p1tbl, k2) 7 times, p1tbl, k9.
**Row 3:** P9, (Wr4, p2) 3 times, Wr4, p9.
**Row 5:** P9, k1tbl, p2, (Wr4, p2) 3 times, k1tbl, p9.
**Row 7:** P9, (Wr4, p2) 3 times, Wr4, p9.
**Row 9:** P9, k1tbl, p2, (Wr4, p2) 3 times, k1tbl, p9.
**Row 11:** P9, (Wr4, p2) 3 times, Wr4, p9.
**Rows 13, 15, and 17:** Work as for Row 1.
**Row 19:** P9, k1tbl, p2, (Wr4, p2) 3 times, k1tbl, p9.
**Row 21:** P9, (Wr4, p2) 3 times, Wr4, p9.
**Row 23:** P9, k1tbl, p2, (Wr4, p2) 3 times, k1tbl, p9.
**Rows 25, 27, and 29:** Work as for Row 1.

**Row 31:** P9, (Wr4, p2) 3 times, Wr4, p9.
**Row 33:** P9, k1tbl, p2, (Wr4, p2) 3 times, k1tbl, p9.
**Row 35:** P9, (Wr4, p2) 3 times, Wr4, p9.
**Row 37:** P9, k1tbl, p2, (Wr4, p2) 3 times, k1tbl, p9.
**Row 39:** P9, (Wr4, p2) 3 times, Wr4, p9.
**Row 40:** K9, (p1tbl, k2) 7 times, p1tbl, k9.

| | |
|---|---|
| ◩ | Twisted knit on RS, twisted purl on WS |
| ⊠ | Purl on RS, knit on WS |
| ▤ | Wr4 = Sl 4 sts to cn and hold in front of work, wrap the yarn clockwise twice around the stitches and then sl the 4 sts to the right needle without knitting them |

Reversible cables are great for throws, scarves and other garments where both sides are visible. The secret is working knit and purl stitches on a reverse stockinette background or as a stand-alone cable.

# NO. 44  REVERSIBLE HAIR BRAID CABLE

**QR codes: C18F Rib and C18B Rib**

This reversible cable has a pattern repeat of 18 stitches and 8 rows. It is repeated five times up on the swatch. It also looks great worked horizontally on the Socks with Reversible Cables (page 142).

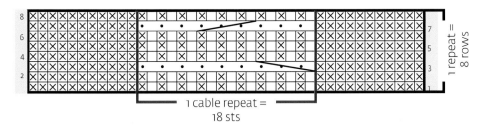

1 cable repeat = 18 sts

CO 40 sts.

**Row 1:** P11, (k1, p1) 9 times, p11.
**Row 2 and all WS rows:** K11, (k1, p1) 9 times, k11.
**Row 3:** P11, C18F Rib, p11.
**Row 5:** Work as for Row 1.
**Row 7:** P11, C18B Rib, p11.
**Row 8:** K11, (k1, p1) 9 times, k11.

Rep Rows 1–8 4 more times = 40 rows.

☐ Knit on RS, purl on WS

☒ Purl on RS, knit on WS

C18F Rib = Sl 6 sts to cn and hold in front of work, work (k1, p1) 3 times; from cn, work (k1, p1) 3 times, work last 6 sts as (k1, p1) 3 times.

C18B Rib = Work (k1, p1) 3 times, sl 6 sts to cn and hold in back of work, work (k1, p1) 3 times; from cn, work (k1, p1) 3 times.

# NO. 45 REVERSIBLE NAUTICAL CABLE

**QR code: C8F Rib**

The chart shows one-and-a-half repeats across and one repeat up; the repeat is worked over 32 stitches and 20 rows. The pattern repeats to form the Curtain Bands on page 124.

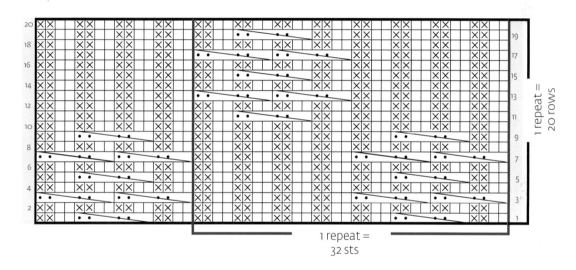

1 repeat =
32 sts

1 repeat =
20 rows

CO 48 sts.

**Row 1:** K2, p2, C8F Rib, (k2, p2) 6 times, C8F Rib, k2, p2.
**Row 2 and all WS rows:** (K2, p2) 12 times.
**Row 3:** (C8F Rib) 2 times, (k2, p2) 4 times, (C8F Rib) 2 times.
**Row 5:** Work as for Row 1.
**Row 7:** Work as for Row 3.
**Row 9:** Work as for Row 1.
**Row 11:** (K2, p2) 5 times, C8F Rib, (k2, p2) 5 times.
**Row 13:** (K2, p2) 4 times, (C8F Rib) 2 times, (k2, p2) 4 times.
**Row 15:** Work as for Row 11.
**Row 17:** Work as for Row 13.
**Row 19:** Work as for Row 11.
**Row 20:** (K2, p2) 12 times.

Rep Rows 1–20 once more = 40 rows.

☐ Knit on RS, purl on WS

☒ Purl on RS, knit on WS

C8F Rib = Sl 4 sts to cn and hold in front of work, k2, p2 and then k2, p2 from cn.

# NO. 46 REVERSIBLE GIANT CABLE

## QR codes: C24F Rib and C24B Rib

The chart shows one repeat across. After the first repeat of the rows up the chart, continue by repeating Rows 1-18. The chart repeat is worked over 48 stitches and 24 rows. See how the cable repeats lengthwise to form Frode's Scarf on page 136.

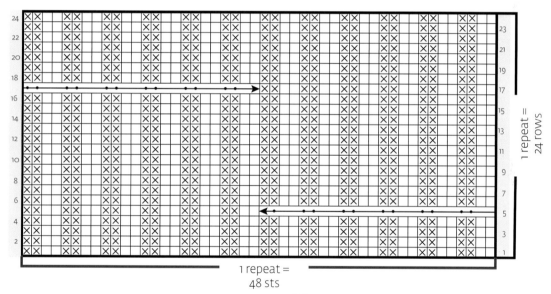

1 repeat = 24 rows

1 repeat = 48 sts

CO 48 sts.

**Rows 1-4:** (K2, p2) 12 times.
**Row 5:** C24F Rib, (k2, p2) 6 times.
**Rows 6-16:** (K2, p2) 12 times.
**Row 17:** (K2, p2) 6 times, C24B Rib.
**Rows 18-24:** (K2, p2) 12 times.

Rep Rows 1-18 once more = 42 rows.

☐  Knit on RS, purl on WS

☒  Purl on RS, knit on WS

C24F Rib = Sl 12 sts to cn and hold in front of work, (k2, p2) 3 times and then (k2, p2) 3 times from cn.

C24B Rib = Sl 12 sts to cn and hold in back of work, (k2, p2) 3 times and then (k2, p2) 3 times from cn.

# Running Cables

I decided to swatch only one running cable pattern. A running cable can best be described as a cable with a certain number of stitches twisted to the right for a certain number of rows and then twisted left the next time. The cables wind side-to-side like a snake instead of weaving over and under each other as for most other cables.

# NO. 47  LITTLE SIDEWINDER CABLE

**QR codes: C2F and C2B**
This swatch shows four identical cable repeats. One cable is worked over 5 stitches and 4 rows. The center stitch is always worked as knit 1 through back loop on the right side and purl 1 through back loop on the wrong side. The cable is featured on the Bolero (see page 165).

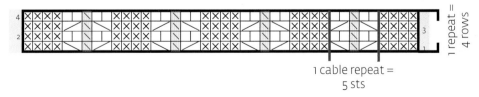

1 cable repeat = 5 sts

1 repeat = 4 rows

CO 40 sts.

**Row 1:** (P4, C2B, k1tbl, C2F) 4 times, p4.
**Row 2:** (K4, p2, p1tbl, p2) 4 times, k4.
**Row 3:** (P4, C2F, k1tbl, C2B) 4 times, p4.
**Row 4:** (K4, p2, p1tbl, p2) 4 times, k4.

Rep Rows 1-4 9 more times = 40 rows.

Twisted knit on RS, twisted purl on WS

Purl on RS, knit on WS

C2F = Sl 1 st to cn and hold in front of work, k1, k1 from cn

C2B = Sl 1 st to cn and hold in back of work, k1, k1 from cn

# Cables with Two Cable Needles

Here's a little test for your patience, but, as with most other things, it gets better with practice. Some lovely thick cables can be produced with this technique so these patterns have earned their place in the book.

# NO. 48 CHAIN CABLE

**QR codes: C9F and C9B**
The swatch shows three identical repeats which are each worked over 9 stitches and 16 rows.

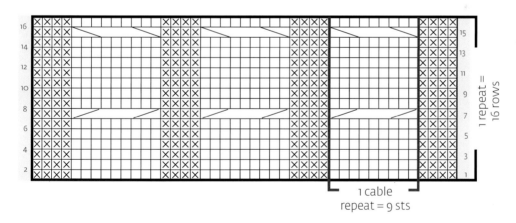

CO 43 sts.

**Rows 1, 3, and 5:** P4, (k9, p4) 3 times.
**Rows 2 and all WS rows:** K4, (p9, k4) 3 times.
**Row 7:** P4, (C9B, p4) 3 times.
**Rows 9, 11, and 13:** P4, (k9, p4) 3 times.
**Row 15:** P4, (C9F, p4) 3 times.
**Row 16:** K4, (p9, k4) 3 times.

Rep Rows 1–16 once more and end with Rows 1–8 = 40 rows.

☐ Knit on RS, purl on WS

☒ Purl on RS, knit on WS

C9B = Sl 3 sts to cn and hold in back of work, sl 3 sts to a second cn and hold in front of work, k3, k3 from front cn, k3 from back cn

C9F = Sl 3 sts to cn and hold in front of work, sl 3 sts to a second cn and hold in back of work, k3, k3 from back cn, k3 from front cn

# NO. 49 FIGURE EIGHT CABLE

**QR code: C9pF**

The swatch shows three identical repeats. The repeats are worked over 9 stitches and 16 rows in a knit 3, purl 3, knit 3 sequence.

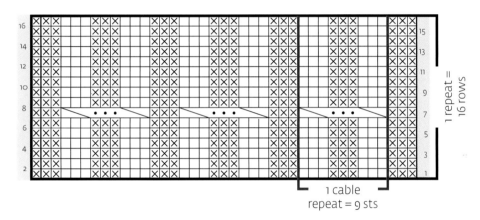

1 repeat = 16 rows

1 cable repeat = 9 sts

CO 39 sts.

**Rows 1, 3, and 5:** P3, (k3, p3) 6 times.
**Rows 2 and all WS rows:** (K3, p3) 6 times, k3.
**Row 7:** P3, (C9pB, p3) 3 times.
**Rows 9, 11, 13, and 15:** P3, (k3, p3) 6 times.
**Row 16:** (K3, p3) 6 times, k3.

Rep Rows 1-16 once more and end with Rows 1-8 = 40 rows.

☐   Knit on RS, purl on WS

☒   Purl on RS, knit on WS

C9pF = Sl 3 sts to cn and hold in front of work, sl 3 purl sts to a second cn and hold in back of work, k3, p3 from back cn, k3 from front cn

# NO. 50 COIN CABLE

**QR code: C9B**
The swatch shows three identical repeats. One cable is worked over 9 stitches and 12 rows.

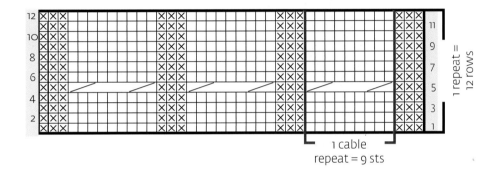

CO 39 sts.

**Rows 1 and 3:** P3, (k9, p3) 3 times.
**Rows 2 and all WS rows:**
(K3, p9) 3 times, k3.
**Row 5:** P3, (C9B, p3) 3 times.
**Rows 7, 9, 11, 13, and 15:** P3,
(k9, p3) 3 times.
**Row 16:** (K3, p9) 3 times, k3.

Rep Rows 1-12 2 more times and end
with Rows 1-4 = 40 rows.

☐ Knit on RS, purl on WS

☒ Purl on RS, knit on WS

C9B = Sl 3 sts to cn and hold in back of work, sl 3 sts to a second cn and hold in front of work, k3, k3 from front cn, k3 from back cn

# GARMENTS, ACCESSORIES, AND HOUSEHOLD ITEMS

## PART 2

In the following pages, you'll find pattern instructions for a variety of items knitted with cables mostly taken from Part 1. Some of the pieces combine several cable patterns and, once you've learned how to knit cables, you can arrange your own pattern combinations for your designs. You'll also find alternate uses for some of the pieces in this section.

## KNITTING TIP

Put a tea-light in a glass that you aren't using for a latte, so the glass cozy becomes a fine tea-light holder. Or, using a soft, pretty alpaca yarn, knit a pair of wrist warmers in the same pattern (see next page). If you knit the wrist warmers with an extra repeat lengthwise, you will have long and elegant cuffs.

# GLASS COZIES

I live over the bakery that my great-grandfather established in 1894 and can get fresh bread every day. On the weekends, it's time for cinnamon buns and other goodies so I can create my own little café. We very much like caffè latte at our house, but the glasses can be too warm to hold comfortably. However, there are no worries with our glass cozies knitted with a good cotton yarn.

## Finished Measurements

**LENGTH:** 5½ in / 14 cm
**CIRCUMFERENCE:** 4 in / 10 cm, when stretched slightly

## Materials

**YARN:** (CYCA #1), Catania Fine from Schachenmayr, 100% cotton (180 yd/165 m / 50 g), 1 ball

Turquoise 253 (enough for two glass cozies)
**NEEDLES:** U.S. size 4 / 3.5 mm + cable needle

CO 50 sts and work back and forth in pattern following the chart until piece is 5½ in / 14 cm long = 1.5 repeats. BO after completing Row 14.

## Finishing

Fold the piece with RS facing RS. Seam the long edges with whip stitch in the outermost stitch on each side. Weave in all ends neatly on WS.

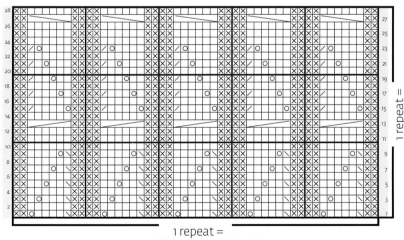

1 repeat =
10 stitches = 50 sts total

1 repeat = 28 rows

| | | |
|---|---|---|
| ☐ | Knit on RS, purl on WS | |
| ☒ | Purl on WS, knit on RS | |
| ◨ | Ssk (or sl 1, k1, psso) | |
| ◪ | K2tog | |

| | |
|---|---|
| ⧂ | Yarnover |
| ⬓ | C6B = Sl 3 sts to cn and hold in back of work, k3, k3 from cn |
| ⬓ | C6F = Sl 3 sts to cn and hold in front of work, k3, k3 from cn |

# BREAKFAST MATS

I think this cable pattern is excellent for breakfast mats. The pattern is easy to memorize and doesn't take a lot of concentration. It's so comfy to have the breakfast table set with these mats. Always slip the first stitch purlwise with the yarn held in front of the work and knit the last stitch of the row through back loop to make a nice edge on each side.

**Finished Measurements**
Approx. 16½ x 12¼ in / 42 x 31 cm

**Materials**
**Yarn:** (CYCA #1), Catania Fine from Schachenmayr, 100% cotton (180 yd/165 m / 50 g), 5 balls Turquoise 253 (for two mats)
**Needles:** U.S. size 8 / 5 mm + cable needle

**Note**: Work with two strands held together throughout.

With two strands of yarn held together, CO 78 sts and work back and forth in seed stitch for 6 rows. Now work following the chart until piece is 11 in / 28 cm

from cast-on row. Work 6 rows in seed st and then BO.

Weave in all ends neatly on WS. Make another mat the same way or as many as you like.

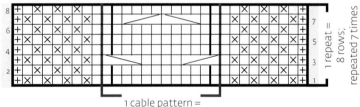

1 repeat =
8 rows;
repeated 7 times

1 cable pattern =
12 stitches; repeated 5 times

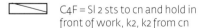

☐ Knit on RS, purl on WS

☒ Purl on WS, knit on RS

⊞ Edge st—sl 1st st purlwise wyf; work last st as k1tbl

⬜ C4F = Sl 2 sts to cn and hold in front of work, k2, k2 from cn

⬜ C4B = Sl 2 sts to cn and hold in back, k2, k2 from cn

Seed Stitch =
**Row 1:** (K1, p1) across.
**Row 2 and all following rows:** Work purl over knit and knit over purl.

# POTHOLDERS

I always need double potholders because I am a master at burning myself on both baking sheets and hot casserole dishes. These potholders are knitted with two identical pieces but in different colors, and in an optical illusion cable pattern. You don't need a cable needle to work these cables.

**Finished Measurements**
Approx. 8¾ x 9½ in / 22 x 24 cm

**Materials**
**Yarn:** (CYCA #3), DROPS Loves You I, 50% cotton, 50% polyester (126 yd/115 m / 50 g)
**Yarn Amounts:**
Light Purple 23, 150 g
White 02, 150 g
OR
**Yarn:** (CYCA # 2), Bjørk from Viking of Norway, 90% cotton, 10% wool (164 yd/150 m / 50 g)
**Yarn Amounts:**
Light Purple 564, 100 g
White 500, 100 g
**Needles:** U.S. size 2.5 / 3 mm
**Crochet Hook:** U.S. size D-3 / 3 mm
**Gauge:** 23 sts in stockinette = 4 in / 10 cm.
Adjust needle size to obtain correct gauge if necessary.

**Note:** The potholders are worked back and forth. Always slip the first st of each row purlwise with yarn in front = edge stitch.

With Light Purple, CO 52 sts and knit 6 rows in garter st. Now work in pattern following the chart, with 8 sts on each side on garter st throughout. Work the row repeat twice (= 56 rows total) and then work 6 rows in garter stitch. BO.

Make the other piece the same way but with White yarn.

**Finishing**
Place the pieces with WS facing WS and sew together using Light Purple yarn through the innermost loop of edge st on each piece. Weave in all ends neatly on WS before you finish seaming.

**Hanging loop:** With crochet hook and Light Purple, insert hook into a corner st and ch 10. Join into a ring with 1 sl st. Work 12 sc around ring and end with 1 sl st into 1st sc. Fasten off yarn.

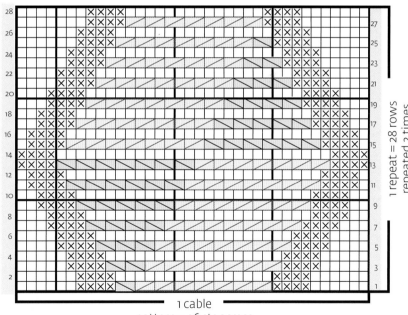

1 cable
pattern = 36 sts across

1 repeat = 28 rows
repeated 2 times

☐   Knit on RS, purl on WS

☒   Purl on WS, knit on RS

◺   Tw1R = K2tog without dropping sts from left needle, insert needle between the 2 sts and knit the 1st st. Sl sts from needle.

◣   Tw1L = Knit 2nd st on left needle through back loop without dropping it from needle; knit the 1st and 2nd sts tog tbl and then slip sts from needle.

## KNITTING TIP

Instead of a loop, add a button to make this into a pretty headband. Be sure to measure the head circumference of the intended recipient so it will fit well. See the photo on the next page.

# CURTAIN BANDS

Here's a reversible cable pattern that's perhaps a little lavish to have on a curtain band. The cable, though, is nice and firm and the yarn has a lovely luster, so I indulged in a double cable.

## Finished Measurements
Approx. 15¾ in / 40 cm long

## Materials
Yarn: (CYCA #2), DROPS Cotton Viscose, 54% cotton, 46% viscose (120 yd/110 m / 50 g), 2 balls color 29

**Needles:** U.S. size 4 / 3.4 mm + cable needle

**Crochet Hook:** U.S. size C-2 / 2.5 mm

CO 56 sts and, work 4 rows back and forth in stockinette. Continue in pattern, following the chart until the piece is approx. 15 in / 38 cm long. Work 4 rows stockinette and then BO. Cut yarn.

## Finishing
Using a strand of Cotton Viscose, baste along the cast-on row and then tighten the yarn to gather in the edge slightly. Gather in bound-off edge the same way.

Crochet loops at the center of the cast-on and bound-off edges. Attach yarn at the center of one short end and ch 12. Join into a ring with 1 sl st into the first ch. Work 18 sc around the ring and then join with 1 sl st to 1st sc. Cut yarn and weave in ends. Make another loop the same way on the opposite short end. Weave in all ends neatly on WS.

☐ Knit on RS, purl on WS

☒ Purl on WS, knit on RS

C8F rib = Sl 4 sts to cn and hold in front of work, k2, p2; k2, p2 from cn

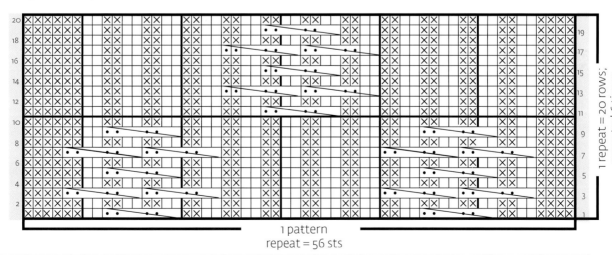

1 pattern repeat = 56 sts

1 repeat = 20 rows; repeated 6 times

# COZY SLIPPERS

I have a tendency to throw my legs up on a hassock when I sit down to knit and watch TV or listen to music in the evening. It's not long before my toes are freezing. For that reason, I always have a pair of cozy slippers in my handwork basket and these keep me quite toasty. I added a thin layer of Sock Stop (latex) on the soles so the slippers won't be slippery. You can buy the latex at hobby shops, some yarn stores, or on the internet.

Repeat = 2 sts

1 repeat = 6 rows

1 cable repeat = 20 sts

☐ Knit on RS, purl on WS

☒ Purl on RS, knit on WS

C6F = Sl 3 sts to cn and hold in front of work, k3, k3 from cn

C6B = Sl 3 sts to cn and hold in back of work, k3, k3 from cn

## Finished Measurements

U.S. shoe sizes 5-6 (7-8, 9½-11, 10½-12) / Euro shoe sizes 35/37 (38/39, 40/42, 43/45)

## Materials

**Yarn:** (CYCA #3), Alpakka Strømpegarn from Sandnes, 70% alpaca, 30% polyamide (120 yd/110 m / 50 g), 3 (3, 4, 4) balls color 4622

**Needles:** U.S. size 4 / 3.5 mm + cable needle

**Crochet Hook:** U.S. size D-3 / 3 mm

**Gauge:** 22 sts in seed st = 4 in / 10 cm.

Adjust needle size to obtain correct gauge if necessary.

**Note:** The slippers are worked back and forth. Work stitches into seed st pattern when increasing or decreasing.

CO 52 (54, 56, 58) sts.

**Row 1:** K2tog, work 14 (15, 16, 17) sts in seed st, 20 sts in cable pattern following chart, 14 (15, 16, 17) seed sts, k2tog.

**Row 2:** Work 15 (16, 17, 18) seed sts, 20 sts cable following chart, 15 (16, 17, 18) seed sts.

Continue in seed st and cable until you've worked 10 rows. Now begin the gusset at the ankle.

## Ankle Gusset

*Work 6 sts, turn and work 6 sts; work 9 sts, turn and work 9 sts; work 12 sts, turn and work 12 sts; work 16 sts, turn and work 16 sts. Work 12 sts, turn and work 12 sts; work 9 sts, turn and work 9 sts; work 6 sts, turn and work 6 sts*. Work 1 row in seed st and cable over all the sts across and then work the gusset, * to * on the opposite side (from the WS). Work 1 row in seed st and cable and then work 10 rows over all the sts.

## Heel Gusset

Work *5 sts, turn and work back, and, *at the same time*, increase 1 st by working 2 sts (k1f&b) into last st of row. Work 7 sts, turn and work back, with k1f&b in the last st. Continue, working 2 more sts each time you turn, and, *at the same time*, increasing in the last st a total of 8 times = 23 (24, 25, 26) sts before the cable. You have completed all the increases at the side but will now continue in short rows with 1 more st each time until you've worked all the sts to the cable. Work 1 row over all the sts before the cable. Next, work the opposite side mirror-image: work 1 st less before turning. When there are 2 (3, 4, 5) sts before the cable, k2tog with the last 2 sts of the row and work 2 fewer sts each time you turn for a total of 8 times = 15 (16, 17, 18) sts before the cable*. Work 1 row over all the sts and the work the gusset, * to * on the opposite side (from the WS).

Work 1 row over all the sts and then pm in the outermost st of the row (on RS). This indicates the point for measuring the foot. Continue in seed st and cable. *At the same time*, shape the foot by decreasing with k2tog on each side of the cable on the RS rows a total of 3 (3, 4, 4) times = 44

(46, 48, 50) sts rem. Continue in pattern over the rem sts until foot measures 6¾ (7, 7½, 8) in / 17 (18, 19, 20) cm from marker.

*Size U.S. 7-8 / Euro 38-39 only:*
On the last row before the toe shaping, k2tog at the center of the cable.

## Toe Shaping

**Row 1:** *Sl 2 sts, k1, p2sso, p1, k1, p1*. Rep * to * across.

**Rows 2-3:** Work in seed st.

**Row 4:** *Sl 2 sts, k1, p2sso, p1, k1, p1*. Rep * to * across.

**Rows 5-6:** Work in seed st.

**Row 7:** K2tog across.

Cut yarn and draw end through rem sts; tighten.

## Finishing

Seam the center of the sole, from the toe and up to the cast-on row, holding the sides edge to edge and stitching through the outermost st loop to avoid a thick seam.

Make the second slipper the same way.

## Edging around Top of Leg

Crochet a picot edge around the top of each slipper:
Beginning at center back, work (ch 3, 1 dc in 1st ch, skip 1 st, 1 sl st into next st) around. Cut yarn and weave in all ends neatly on WS.

# THROW

Throws are cozy! I knitted this throw in different colors as a gift to my son when he moved into a new apartment. However, there was someone else who clearly wanted a blanket—our kitty cat Lillefix. He loves to bury himself and twist around until he's comfy in the throw.

## Finished Measurements
Approx. 39½ x 51¼ in /
100 x 130 cm

## Materials
**Yarn:** (CYCA #5), Hexa from Du Store Alpakka, 100% alpaca (109 yd/100 m / 50 g)

**Yarn Amounts:**
Blue 922 (Color A), 300 g
Natural 910 (Color B), 250 g
Beige 911 (Color C), 550 g

**Needles:** U.S. size 10 / 6 mm + cable needle

**Crochet Hook:** U.S. size J-10 / 6 mm

**Gauge:** 17 sts in stockinette st = 4 in / 10 cm.
Adjust needle size to obtain correct gauge if necessary.

**Notes:** The throw is worked in five strips that are then sewn together (see schematic on page 130). Three of the strips consist of three color blocks and the two narrower strips feature cables. For the three strips of blocks, the edge stitches are not included on the chart.

## Strip 1
With Color C, CO 50 sts and work following Chart 3, with an edge st (knit on all rows) at each side. Work the repeat a total of 7 times.
Change to Color B and work following Chart 2, working the repeat a total of 7 times. Change to Color A and work Chart 1 for a total of 7 repeats. Repeat these three blocks once more. BO and set piece aside.

## Strip 2
With Color A, CO 50 sts and work following Chart 1, with an edge st (knit on all rows) at each side. Work the repeat a total of 7 times.
Change to Color C and work Chart 3 a total of 7 times. Change to Color B and work Chart 2 a total of 7 times. Repeat these three blocks once more. BO and set piece aside.

## Strip 3
With Color B, CO 50 sts and work Chart 2, with an edge st (knit on all rows) at each side, a total of 7 times.
Change to Color A and repeat Chart 1 a total of 7 times. Change to Color C and work following Chart 3, repeating the rows a total of 7 times. Repeat these three blocks once more. BO and set piece aside.

## Strips 4 and 5: Cables
With Color A, CO 30 sts and work following Chart 4. Work the repeat a total of 8 times. BO and set piece aside. Make another cable strip the same way.

## Finishing
Begin with Strip 1 and one of the cable strips. Place the pieces with RS sides facing. With Color A, use whip stitch to join the strips through the outermost stitch loop on each piece. Sew Strip 2 to the opposite side of the cable strip. Attach the 2nd cable strip and then the 3rd block strip. Weave in all ends neatly on WS.

## Edging
**Rnd 1:** Work (2 sc, skip 1 st) around.
**Rnd 2:** Working in each st around, work crab stitch (= single crochet worked from left to right).

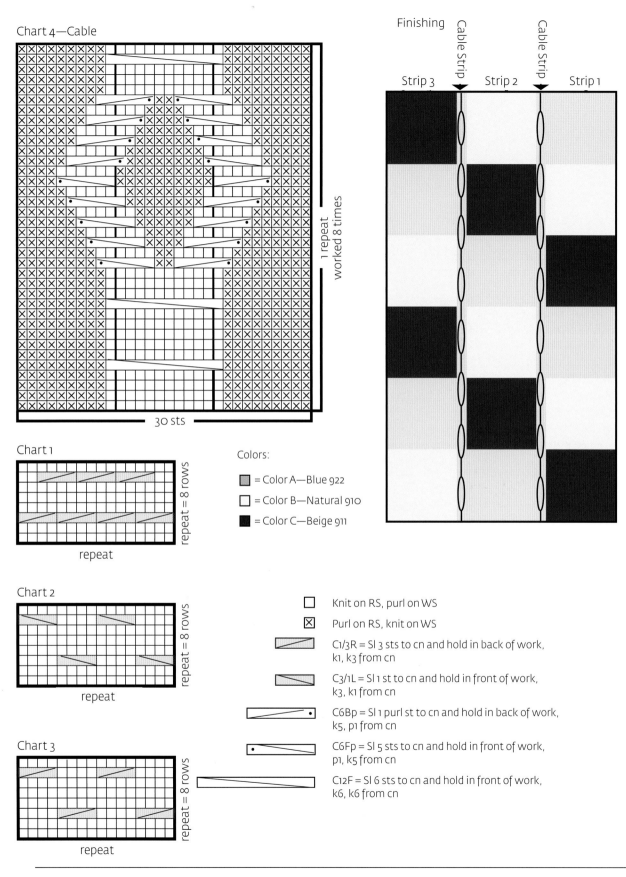

Chart 4—Cable

1 repeat
worked 8 times

30 sts

Finishing

Strip 3 | Cable Strip | Strip 2 | Cable Strip | Strip 1

Chart 1

repeat = 8 rows

repeat

Colors:

■ = Color A—Blue 922

□ = Color B—Natural 910

■ = Color C—Beige 911

Chart 2

repeat = 8 rows

repeat

Chart 3

repeat = 8 rows

repeat

□ Knit on RS, purl on WS

☒ Purl on RS, knit on WS

C1/3R = Sl 3 sts to cn and hold in back of work,
k1, k3 from cn

C3/1L = Sl 1 st to cn and hold in front of work,
k3, k1 from cn

C6Bp = Sl 1 purl st to cn and hold in back of work,
k5, p1 from cn

C6Fp = Sl 5 sts to cn and hold in front of work,
p1, k5 from cn

C12F = Sl 6 sts to cn and hold in front of work,
k6, k6 from cn

# HAT, COWL, MITTENS, AND LEG WARMERS

I think this set is really super. I tried on the leg warmers to see if they fit and they warmed my whole body right away. The same cable appears on each of these accessories except for the cowl which has an extra wide cable composed of two adjoining cables.

**Size Women's,** one size

**Materials**
**Yarn:** (CYCA #5), Hexa from Du Store Alpakka, 100% alpaca (109 yd/100 m / 50 g), color 923
**Yarn Amounts:**
Hat (fits head circumference 20½-22 in / 52-56 cm), 100 g
Mittens, 100 g
Cowl, 100 g
Leg Warmers, 100 g
**Needles:** U.S. sizes 8 and 10 / 5 and 6 mm: short circular and set of 5 dpn + cable needle. The smaller needles are for the mittens only; other accessories use the larger size throughout.
**Gauge**: 16 sts in stockinette st on larger needles = 4 in / 10 cm. Adjust needle sizes to obtain correct gauge if necessary.

**Cowl**
**Measurements, before finishing:** length 22¾ in / 58 cm, wide, 6¼ in / 16 cm

With U.S. size 10 / 6 mm needles, CO 46 sts and work charted pattern for the cowl (see page 135) until piece is 22¾ in / 58 cm long. BO.

**Finishing**
With WS facing, seam short ends of cowl with RS facing you so that you can make sure the cables align as you stitch. Weave in ends neatly on WS.

**Hat**
With U.S. size 10 / 6 mm needles, CO 24 sts and work in charted pattern (see page 135) until piece measures 20½ in / 52 cm. BO and seam the short ends. With short circular, pick up and knit 110 sts along one long edge (into the purl sts). Join and purl 1 rnd and then work around in stockinette for 2½ in / 6 cm. Shape crown as follows:
Pm after every 22nd st. [Knit until 1 st before marker, sl 2 knitwise (as if to knit together), k1, p2sso] around = 10 sts decreased. Knit 1 rnd. Decrease as before on every other round with 2 fewer sts between decreases until 10 sts rem. Cut yarn and draw end through rem sts; tighten well. Weave in ends neatly on WS.

**Leg Warmers**
**Finished Measurements:**
Length 16½ in / 42 cm; width, 5½ in / 14 cm

**Right Leg Warmer**
With U.S. size 10 / 6 mm needles, CO 64 sts and work 32 sts in k1, p1 ribbing and then work 32 sts of chart for right leg warmer (see page 135). Continue as set until piece is 16½ in / 42 cm long. BO and weave in ends neatly on WS.

**Left Leg Warmer**
With U.S. size 10 / 6 mm needles, CO 64 sts and work 32 sts in k1, p1 ribbing and then work 32 sts of chart for left leg warmer (see page 135). Continue as set until piece is 16½ in / 42 cm long. BO and weave in ends neatly on WS.

**Finishing**
Fold each leg warmer lengthwise and, with right sides facing, seam. Turn right side out and wear with cable at the front of the leg and the seam at one side.

**Mittens**
The mittens are worked back and forth on U.S. size 8 / 5 mm needles.

**Left Mitten**
CO 42 sts. With the outermost st at each side as an edge st, work charted ribbing (5 rep across)

for 3½ in / 9 cm. Continue in stockinette and cable following the chart for the left mitten. *At the same time*, shape the thumb gusset: Work 18 sts, M1, k2, M1, k2, pattern following the chart over 16 sts, k4. Turn and work 1 row. Increase on the next row by working 19 sts, M1, k4, M1, k2, cable over 16 sts, k4. Turn and work 1 row. Continue increasing the same way until there are 10 sts for the thumb. Place these 10 sts on a holder and complete row. On the next row, CO 2 sts over gap = 42 sts total. Continue in stockinette and charted pattern. When piece measures 8 in / 20 cm from cast-on row, shape top.

Shape top of the mitten. Work in stockinette over all the sts.

**Decrease Row 1 (RS):** (K2, k2tog) across, ending with k2. Purl 1 row.
**Decrease Row 2:** (K1, k2tog) across, ending with k2. Purl 1 row.
**Decrease Row 3:** K2tog across. Cut yarn and draw end through rem sts; tighten.

## Thumb
Place the 10 sts set aside for thumb onto dpn U.S. size 8 / 5 mm; pick up and knit 4 sts across top of thumbhole. The first row will be a little tight. Work the thumb back and forth in stockinette for about 2 in / 5 cm. Shape tip of thumb as for top of mitten. Cut yarn and draw end through rem sts; tighten.

## Right Mitten
Work as for left mitten but mirror-image. After completing the ribbing, place thumbhole as follows:
K4, 16 sts charted pattern, k2, M1, k2, M1, k18. Turn and work 1 row. On the next row: work 19 sts, M1, k4, M1, k2, 16 sts charted pattern, k4. Turn and work 1 row. Continue increasing the same way until there are 10 sts for thumb. Continue and finish as for left mitten.

## Finishing
With WS facing, seam each mitten with whip stitch in the outermost stitch loop at each side. Seam thumb. Weave in all ends neatly on WS.

## Chart for Cowl

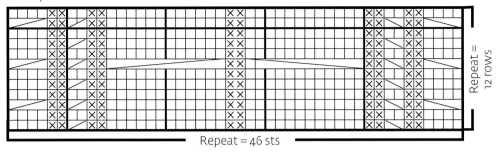

Repeat = 12 rows

Repeat = 46 sts

### Mitten Ribbing

1 repeat = 12 rows

## Chart for left leg warmer, hat and left mitten

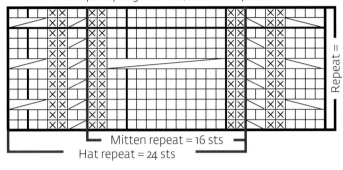

Repeat = 12 rows

Mitten repeat = 16 sts

Hat repeat = 24 sts

## Chart for right leg warmer and right mitten

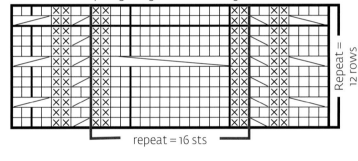

Repeat = 12 rows

repeat = 16 sts

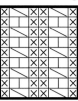

☐ Knit on RS, purl on WS

☒ Purl on RS, knit on WS

C2F = Sl 1 st to cn and hold in front of work, k1, k1 from cn

C2B = Sl 1 st to cn and hold in back of work, k1, k1 from cn.

C4F = Sl 2 sts to cn and hold in front of work, k2, k2 from cn.

C4B = Sl 2 sts to cn and hold in back of work, k2, k2 from cn.

C12F = Sl 6 sts to cn and hold in front of work, k6, k6 from cn.

C12B = Sl 6 sts to cn and hold in back of work, k6, k6 from cn.

# FRODE'S SCARF

This scarf is knitted with reversible cables. There is no wrong side and both sides look just as good. The scarf is great for both women and men but it was especially nice on Frode.

**Size** One size

**Total Length:** approx. 64½ in / 164 cm

**Materials**
**YARN:** (CYCA #4), Carpe Diem from Lang Yarns, 70% Merino wool, 30% alpaca (98 yd/90 m / 50 g), 5 balls color 714

**NEEDLES:** U.S. size 10 / 6 mm: short circular + cable needle.
**GAUGE:** 26 sts in k2, p2 ribbing = 4 in / 10 cm.
Adjust needle size to obtain correct gauge if necessary.

CO 48 sts and work 2 rows k2, p2 ribbing. Now work following the chart on the next page. Pm

on the row where you cross the cables so that it will be easier to count for a right- or left-leaning cable on every 12th row.

Work until the scarf is about 63 in / 160 cm long and then work 4 rows k2, p2 ribbing. BO in ribbing.

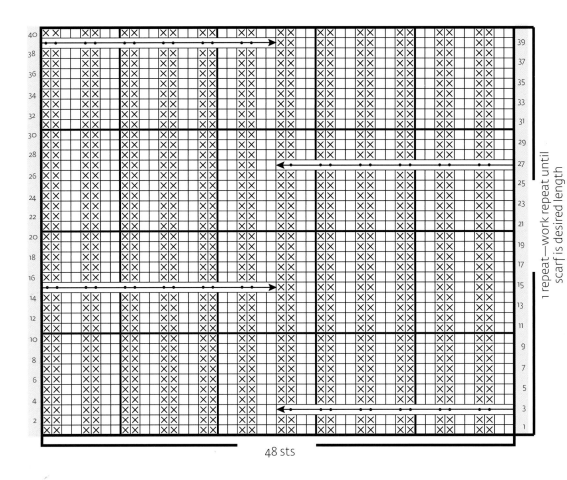

48 sts

1 repeat—work repeat until scarf is desired length

□  Knit on RS, purl on WS

☒  Purl on RS, knit on WS

C24F Rib = Sl 12 sts to cn and hold in front of work, (k2, p2) 3 times and then, from cn, work (k2, p2) 3 times

C24B Rib = Sl 12 sts to cn and hold in back of work, (k2, p2) 3 times and then, from cn, work (k2, p2) 3 times

# CARPENTER'S COMFORTS

I happily followed the complete construction process when we built a new cabin. The carpenter worked in all kinds of weather and I often thought about how a fluttery scarf could easily get caught in a saw or otherwise be in the way. Holding the hammer and nails must also have contributed to cold hands. Wrist warmers aren't just for women, so I knitted a cowl and wrist warmers set for the carpenter.

**Size** One size

## Materials
**Yarn:** (CYCA #4), Alpakka Ull (alpaca wool) from Sandnes, 65% alpaca, 35% wool (109 yd/100 m / 50 g), 2 balls color 6052
**Needles:** U.S. size 8 / 5 mm: straights + an extra for finishing + cable needle.
**Crochet Hook:** U.S. size G-6 / 4 mm
**Gauge:** 21 sts in cable pattern = 4 in / 10 cm.
Adjust needle size to obtain correct gauge if necessary.

## Cowl
CO 42 sts and work back and forth in charted pattern until piece measures approx. 22¾ in / 58 cm. Do not bind off.

## Finishing
With an extra needle, pick up and knit 42 sts partially along the long side (see drawing on page 141). Hold the needle parallel to the short edge and join the pieces with three-needle bind-off. Work around in sc on both top and bottom edges of the cowl.

Wrist Warmers (work the entire chart)

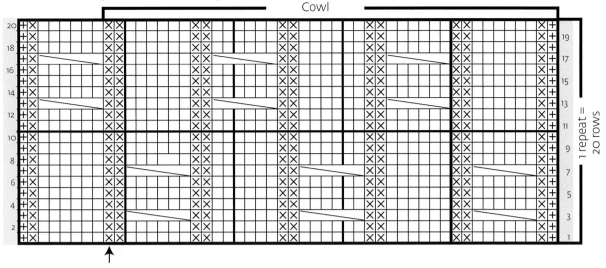

Cowl

1 repeat = 20 rows

↑
Change this line of stitches to
an edge st for the cowl

| + | Knit on RS, knit on WS |
| □ | Knit on RS, purl on WS |
| ⊠ | Purl on RS, knit on WS |
| ╱ | C6F = Sl 3 sts to cn and hold in front of work, k3, k3 from cn |

Cowl—Finishing

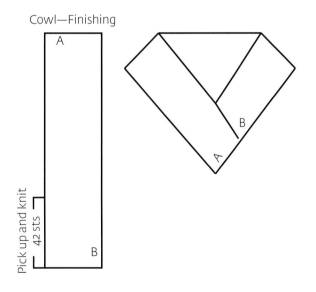

## Wrist Warmers

CO 50 sts and work in charted pattern until piece is approx. 8 in / 20 cm long. BO. Make both alike.

### Finishing

Seam the side, leaving an opening for the thumb as follows: With RS facing RS, sew about ¾ in / 2 cm down from the top edge, working into the outermost stitch loops. Cut yarn and fasten off. Skip 2½ in / 6 cm and seam down to bottom edge of wrist warmer. Work sc around the thumbhole and join with 1 sl st into 1st sc. Work in sc around top and bottom edges of wrist warmer.

Make another wrist warmer the same way.

# SOCKS WITH REVERSIBLE CABLES

These socks are knitted with cables that are the same on both sides. Fold down the cabled edge and—VOILÀ!—you have an equally fine cable cuff but a shorter sock. So smart, right?

**Sizes** U.S. shoe sizes 5½-6½ (7½-8) / European sizes 36/37 (38/39)

## Materials
**Yarn:** (CYCA #3), Sterk from Du Store Alpakka, 40% Merino wool, 40% alpaca, 20% nylon (150 yd/137 m / 50 g), 100 g color 834
**Needles:** U.S. size 4 / 3.5 mm: set of 5 dpn + cable needle
**Gauge:** 22 sts in stockinette = 4 in / 10 cm.
Adjust needle size to obtain correct gauge if necessary.

## Cabled Cuff
The cuff is worked back and forth.
CO 26 sts and work in pattern following the chart. Work a total of 10 (11) cables. BO 25 sts and do not cut yarn; keep last st on needle.

## Leg
Pick up and knit a total of 52 (56) sts along long edge of cuff, including the last st from cuff. Divide sts onto 4 dpn = 13 (14) sts on each needle. Join and work in stockinette until leg measures 4¼ in / 11 cm from row of picked-up sts. Decrease 4 sts with k2tog at the beginning of each needle = 48 (52) sts rem.

## Heel Flap
Pm on the center st of the back of the sock and place 12 (13) sts on each side of the marker on a dpn = 24 (26) sts. Work back and forth

in stockinette for a total of 14 (16) rows, ending with a purl row.
*Heel Gusset:* Knit until 10 (11) sts rem on needle, ssk, k1; turn. Purl until 10 (11) sts rem on needle, p2tog, p1; turn. Continue working back and forth with 1 less st on each row until all the sts have been worked. Purl the last row on WS. Divide the rem sts onto 2 dpn (= Needles 1 and 4).

## Gusset
With Needle 1, pick up and knit 12 (14) sts along one side of heel flap; work in stockinette across Needles 2 and 3 (= instep); for Needle 4, pick up and knit 16 (18) sts on other side of flap and knit to center of sole.
### Shape Gusset:
**Rnd 1:**
*Needle 1:* Knit until 2 sts rem, k2tog.
*Needles 2 and 3:* Knit across.
*Needle 4:* Ssk, knit to end of needle.

**Rnd 2: Knit.**
Rep Rnds 1-2 until 48 (52) sts rem (same number as end of leg).

## Foot
Continue around in stockinette until foot measures 7 (7½) in / 18 (19) cm.

## Toe Shaping
**Rnd 1:**
*Needle 1:* Knit until 3 sts rem, k2tog, k1.
*Needle 2:* K1, ssk, knit to end of needle.
*Needle 3:* Work as for Needle 1.
*Needle 4:* Work as for Needle 2.
**Rnd 2: Knit.**
Rep Rnds 1-2 until 14 (16) sts rem. Divide sts onto 2 dpn with 7 (8) sts on each. Turn sock with WS out and carefully pull needles and yarn inside. Hold the needles parallel and join with three-needle bind-off.

Make second sock the same way.

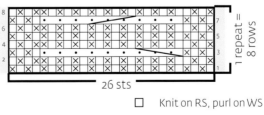

26 sts

1 repeat = 8 rows

☐ Knit on RS, purl on WS

☒ Purl on RS, knit on WS

C18F Rib = Sl 6 sts to cn and hold in front of work, work (k1, p1) 3 times; from cn, work (k1, p1) 3 times; (k1, p1) 3 times over last 6 sts.

C18B Rib = Work (k1, p1) 3 times; sl 6 sts to cn and hold in back of work, work (k1, p1) 3 times; from cn, work (k1, p1) 3 times.

# BOOT TOPPERS

A while ago I translated a fun English book called *20 to Make—Boot Cuffs*. It inspired me to design these boot toppers in a firm cable pattern. They're really warm, to boot!

**Size** One size

**Materials**

**YARN:** (CYCA #2), Lima from Bergère de France, 80% brushed wool, 20% alpaca (120 yd/110 m / 50 g), 2 balls color 20441

**NEEDLES:** U.S. size 4 / 3.5 mm + cable needle

**GAUGE:** 32 sts in cable pattern = 4 in / 10 cm.

Adjust needle size to obtain correct gauge if necessary.

**NOTE:** The boot toppers are worked back and forth.

CO 64 sts and work in k2, p2 ribbing until piece measures 4 in / 10 cm. On the next row, increase 16 sts evenly spaced across (M1 after every 4th st) = 80 sts. Knit 1

row on WS (= foldline) and then continue in charted pattern until the cable section is 4 in / 10 cm long. End with a RS row and then BO knitwise on WS.

**Finishing**

With WS facing you, seam the sides of the section with the cables, using whip stitch. Turn work right side out and seam the ribbed section.

Weave in all ends neatly on WS.

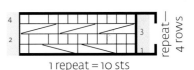

1 repeat = 10 sts

**NOTE:** On Row 1, k2, C4F, and then repeat C4F until 2 sts rem. End with k2.

☐    Knit on RS, purl on WS

C4F = Sl 2 sts to cn and hold in front of work, k2, k2 from cn

C4B = Sl 2 sts to cn and hold in back of work, k2, k2 from cn

# MAJ'S ANKLE SOCKS

Many years ago a very nice older woman lived in the apartment above ours. She was a widow who was often alone but always very comforted by her knitting. Those of us in the apartment below knew this well because she gifted us with the most wonderful socks. One day she came down with a pair of unbelievably elegant ankle socks, knitted on fine needles, with a charming pattern. I had them for many years but, finally, they wore out. I spent a few hours trying to discover how they were knitted and was super happy when I finally cracked the code. Here's the result!

**Sizes** U.S. shoe sizes 5½-6½ (7½-8) / European sizes 36/37 (38/39)

## Materials
**YARN:** (CYCA #1), Gepard Cash socks (strong sock yarn), 69% Merino wool, 25% acrylic, 6% cashmere (224 yd/205 m / 50 g), 100 (100) g color 6006
**NEEDLES:** U.S. size 2.5 / 3 mm: set of 5 dpn + cable needle.
**Gauge:** 30 sts in stockinette or 32 sts in pattern = 4 in / 10 cm. Adjust needle size to obtain correct gauge if necessary.

## Leg
CO 56 (64) sts and divide sts onto 4 dpn = 14 (16) sts on each needle. Join and work in charted pattern until leg measures 3½ in / 9 cm = 7 repeats. Cut yarn.

## Heel Flap
The heel flap is worked over the sts on Needles 4 and 1. Work back and forth in stockinette over 28 (32) sts for a total of 18 (20) rows, ending with 1 purl row on WS.
**Heel Gusset:** Knit until 10 (11) sts rem on needle, ssk, k1; turn. Purl until 10 (11) sts rem on needle, p2tog, p1; turn. Continue working back and forth with 1 less st on each row until all the

sts have been worked. Purl the last row on WS. Divide the rem sts onto 2 dpn (= Needles 1 and 4).

## Gusset
With Needle 1, pick up and knit 16 (18) sts along one side of heel flap; work in stockinette across Needles 2 and 3 (= instep); pick up and knit 16 (18) sts on other side of flap with Needle 4 and knit to center of sole.
### Shape Gusset:
**Rnd 1:**
*Needle 1:* Knit until 2 sts rem, k2tog.
*Needles 2 and 3:* Knit across.
*Needle 4:* Ssk, knit to end of needle.
**Rnd 2:** Knit.
Rep Rnds 1-2 until 56 (64) sts rem (same number as end of leg).

## Foot
Continue around in stockinette until foot measures 7 (7½) in / 18 (19) cm.

## Toe Shaping
**Rnd 1:**
*Needle 1:* Knit until 3 sts rem, k2tog, k1.
*Needle 2:* K1, ssk, knit to end of needle.
*Needle 3:* Work as for Needle 1.

*Needle 4:* Work as for Needle 2.

**Rnd 2: Knit.**
Rep Rnds 1-2 until 14 (16) sts rem. Divide sts onto 2 dpn with 7 (8) on each. Turn sock with WS out and carefully pull needles and yarn inside. Hold the needles parallel and, with a third dpn, join with three-needle bind-off.

Make second sock the same way.

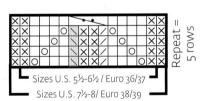

Repeat = 5 rows

Sizes U.S. 5½-6½ / Euro 36/37
Sizes U.S. 7½-8/ Euro 38/39

| | |
|---|---|
| ☐ | Knit |
| ☒ | Purl |
| ⊙ | Yarnover |
| ╱ | K2tog |
| ╲ | K2tog tbl |
| ⟋•• | C4Fp = Sl 1 knit and 2 purl sts to cn and hold in front of work, k1, sl the 2 purl sts to left needle and purl them, k1 from cn |

# TORMOD'S STOCKINGS

My beloved goes on guy outings several times a year. He has been a scout since his boyhood and he and several life-long friends like to join up and go on various trips—either to a cabin or with a tent. I think that he has earned some special socks that he can show off before the fireplace or a long ski run. I suspect the other guys are green with envy.

**Sizes** U.S. men's shoe sizes 9-11 (12-14) / European sizes 42/44 (45/47)

## Materials
**YARN:** (CYCA #4), Alpakka Ull (alpaca wool) from Sandnes, 65% alpaca, 35% wool (109 yd/100 m / 50 g), 4 balls color 6052
**NEEDLES:** U.S. size 6 / 4 mm: set of 5 dpn, short circular for socks + cable needle. (The ball band suggests a larger size needle but I prefer socks to be knit a little tighter.)
**GAUGE:** 21 sts in cable pattern = 4 in / 10 cm.
Adjust needle size to obtain correct gauge if necessary.

**NOTE:** Both sizes have the same number of stitches but the foot on the larger size is ¾ in / 2 cm longer.

## Leg
With short circular, CO 66 sts. Join and work in k3, p3 ribbing for 3¼ in / 8 cm. Continue in charted pattern until leg measures 9¾ in / 25 cm.

**NOTE:** On the charted pattern, the repeat shifts by 2 stitches on Rows 4 and 10.
On the next rnd, decrease by working p3tog over each set of purl sts = 55 sts. Continue in pattern until leg measures 13½ in / 34 cm. On the next rnd, decrease 7 sts as follows:
P2, k3, p3, k3, (p2tog, k3) 7 times and end with p2, k3, p2, k3 = 48 sts rem. Cut yarn.

## Heel Flap
The heel flap is worked back and forth in stockinette over 24 sts = place 12 sts from left side of circular and 12 sts from right side onto a dpn. Beginning on RS, work 13 rows in stockinette.
**Heel Gusset:**
**Row 1 (WS):** Sl 1 purlwise, purl to end of row.
**Row 2:** Sl 1 purlwise, k13, ssk, k1; turn.
**Row 3:** Sl 1 purlwise, p5, p2tog, p1; turn.
**Row 4:** Sl 1 purlwise, k6, ssk, k1; turn.
**Row 5:** Sl 1 purlwise, p7, p2tog, p1; turn.
**Row 6:** Sl 1 purlwise, k8, ssk, k1; turn.
**Row 7:** Sl 1 purlwise, p9, p2tog, p1; turn.

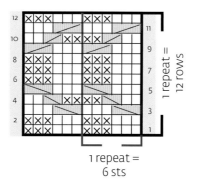

| | |
|---|---|
| ☐ | Knit |
| ☒ | Purl |
| ◹ | Tw1pL = Sl 1 st to cn and hold in front of work, p1, p1 from cn |
| ◿ | Tw1pR = Sl 1 st to cn and hold in back of work, p1, p1 from cn |
| ◹ | C2/1L = Sl 1 st to cn and hold in front of work, k2, k1 from cn |
| ◿ | C1/2R = Sl 2 sts to cn and hold in back of work, k1, k2 from cn |

1 repeat = 12 rows

1 repeat = 6 sts

**Row 8:** Sl 1 purlwise, k10, ssk, k1; turn.

**Row 9:** Sl 1 purlwise, p11, p2tog, p1; turn.

**Row 10:** Sl 1 purlwise, k12, ssk, k1; turn.

**Row 11:** Sl 1 purlwise, p12, p2tog; turn = 14 sts rem. Cut yarn.

### Gusset

The foot is worked with sts divided over 4 dpn. Sl 7 of the 14 heel sts to a dpn = Needle 1 and, with same dpn, pick up and knit 11 sts along left side of heel flap. Sl 12 sts to Needle 2 and 12 sts to Needle 3 = instep. With Needle 4, pick up and knit 11 sts along right side of flap and then k7 from heel. You should have 18 sts each on Needles 1 and 4 and 12 sts each on Needles 2 and 3.

The rest of the sock is worked in stockinette.

### Shape Gusset:
**Rnd 1:**

*Needle 1:* Knit until 3 sts rem, k2tog, k1.

*Needles 2 and 3:* Knit across.

*Needle 4:* K1, ssk, knit to end of needle.

**Rnd 2:** Knit.

Rep Rnds 1-2 5 more times = 12 sts decreased and 48 sts rem (12 sts on each dpn).

### Foot

Continue around in stockinette until foot measures 8¾ (9½) in / 22 (24) cm from heel.

### Toe Shaping
**Rnd 1:**

*Needle 1:* Knit until 3 sts rem, k2tog, k1.

*Needle 2:* K1, ssk, knit to end of needle.

*Needle 3:* Work as for Needle 1.

*Needle 4:* Work as for Needle 2.

**Rnd 2:** Knit.

Rep Rnds 1-2 until 6 sts rem on each dpn.

Sl the first 6 sts to a dpn; the next 12 sts on next dpn and the last 6 sts to 1st dpn. Now put each set of sts onto a large safety pin or waste yarn. Turn the sock inside out and return sts to their respective needles. Hold the needles parallel and, using a third dpn, join with three-needle bind-off. Weave in all ends neatly on WS.

Make the second sock the same way.

## KNITTING TIP

This poncho can also be worn as a bell-shaped skirt. It fits sizes 10/12 (14/16) and Small. You might want to sew in an elastic band so it will fit well at the waist.

# SIGRID'S PONCHO

Little girls love to dress up. When I asked my great niece what her favorite knitted garment was, her top choice was a poncho. This poncho is knitted from the neckband down.

**Sizes** 2-4 (6-8, 10-12) years

### Materials

**YARN:** (CYCA #3), Alpakka from Sandnes, 100% alpaca (120 yd/110 m / 50 g), 5 (5, 6) balls color 7212

**NEEDLES:** U.S. size 4 / 3.5 mm: short and long circulars + cable needle

**CROCHET HOOK:** U.S. size D-3 / 3 mm

**GAUGE:** 26 sts in ribbed cable = 4 in / 10 cm.
Adjust needle size to obtain correct gauge if necessary.

With shorter circular, CO 100 (104, 108) sts; join, being careful not to twist cast-on row. Pm for beg of rnd. Work in pattern following the chart for chosen size = 50 (52, 54) sts per repeat (so work the repeat twice across).

Pay attention to the increases on the chart and work all new sts into pattern with the small cables over two stitches. Change to longer circular when the stitches are too crammed on short circular. Continue in pattern until there are 344 (356, 388) sts total = about 15¾ (18¼, 20½) in / 40 (46, 52) cm. BO in pattern, that is, with knit over knit and purl over purl.

### Edging around neck and lower edge

Crochet 1 rnd of single crochet and then a round of crab st (sc worked from left to right) around each edge.

### Finishing

Weave in all ends neatly on WS. Gently steam press on WS.

| | |
|---|---|
| ☐ | Knit |
| ☒ | Purl |
| ▼ | Increase 1 st |
| ⬱ | C2F = Sl 1 st to cn and hold in front of work, k1, k1 from cn |
| ⬱ | C4B = Sl 2 sts to cn and hold in back of work, k2, k2 from cn |
| ⬱ | C4Bp = Sl 2 sts to cn and hold in back of work, p2, k2 from cn |
| ⬱ | C4Fp = Sl 2 sts to cn and hold in front of work, k2, p2 from cn |

Continue with pattern and increases

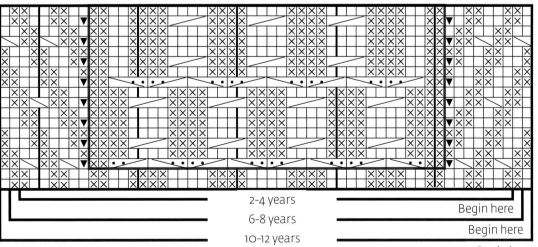

2-4 years
6-8 years
10-12 years
Begin here
Begin here
Begin here

The pattern sequence is repeated once more for all sizes

## KNITTING TIP

If you knit this pullover a little longer, it can be worn by a woman as a tunic (see photo on page opposite Contents page).

# PULLOVER FOR PETTER

Those who know me well know that all shades of aqua, mint, and turquoise are my absolute favorite colors. There were a few, though, who were a little surprised that I knitted a man's vest in fine silk and alpaca, but shouldn't the guys also have a bit of exclusive quality—in my favorite color?

**Sizes** S (M, L, XL, XXL, XXXL)

## Finished Measurements
**Chest:** 35½ (39½, 43¼, 47¼, 51¼, 55¼) in / 90 (100, 110, 120, 130, 140) cm
**Length:** 25¼ (26, 26, 26¾, 26¾, 27½) in / 64 (66, 66, 68, 68, 70) cm

## Materials
**Yarn:** (CYCA #1), Alpakka Silke from Sandnes, 70% alpaca, 30% silk (218 yd/199 m / 50 g), 5 (6, 6, 7, 7, 8) balls color 7212
**Needles:** U.S. size 2.5 / 3 mm + cable needle.
**Gauge:** 28 sts in pattern, slightly stretched = 4 in / 10 cm.
Adjust needle size to obtain correct gauge if necessary.

**Note:** The garment is worked back and forth.

## Back
CO 116 (128, 144, 152, 168, 180) sts and work 1 row in twisted knit sts for a smooth edge. Now work charted pattern 1 for 2¾ in / 7 cm. Change to charted pattern 2 and work until piece measures 9¾ (10¼, 10¼, 10¾, 10¾, 11) in / 25 (26, 26, 27, 27, 28) cm. Begin increasing 1 st at each side every 1½ in / 4 cm a total of 5 times = 126 (138, 154, 162, 178, 190) sts. Work the new sts into pattern. When piece measures 17¾ (18¼, 18¼, 18½, 18½,

19) in / 45 (46, 46, 47, 47, 48) cm, BO 5 sts at each side for armholes = 116 (128, 144, 152, 168, 180) sts. Continue in pattern until piece measures 24½ (25¼, 25¼, 26, 26, 26¾) in / 62 (64, 64, 66, 66, 68) cm. Place the center 50 (52, 54, 56, 58, 60) sts on a holder and work each side separately. At neck edge, BO 2 sts once, 1 st 3 times for all sizes = 28 (33, 40, 43, 50, 55) sts rem for shoulder. BO rem sts and work the other side the same way.

## Front
Work as for the back until front measures 23¾ (24½, 24½, 25¼, 25¼, 26) in / 60 (62, 62, 64, 64, 66) cm. Place the center 32 (34, 36, 38, 40, 42) sts on a holder and work each side separately. At neck edge, BO 3 sts once, 2 sts 3 times, and 1 st 5 times for all sizes = 28 (33, 40, 43, 50, 55) sts rem for shoulder. BO rem sts and work the other side the same way.

## Finishing
Gently steam press pieces on WS. Seam shoulders.

## Neck and Armhole Bands
Pick up and knit about 120–150 sts (a multiple of 4 sts) around armhole and work back and forth in ribbing

following Chart 1 for ¾ in / 2 cm. BO loosely with knit over knit and purl over purl.
Work both armholes alike. Place the held sts for back neck on needle and work across them, pick up and knit sts on side of neck, work held sts for front neck, pick up and knit sts along opposite side of neck (make sure the stitch counts match). Work in pattern on Chart 1 for 1¼ in / 3 cm and then BO loosely with knit over knit and purl over purl. Seam short ends of neck and armhole bands.
Weave in all ends neatly on WS.

| | |
|---|---|
| ☐ | Knit on RS, purl on WS |
| ☒ | Purl on RS, knit on WS |
| ◹ | C2F = *On RS*, sl 1 st to cn and hold in front of work, k1, k1 from cn<br>*On WS*, sl 1 st to cn and hold in front of work, p1, p1 from cn |

Chart 1

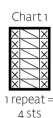

1 repeat = 4 sts

Chart 2

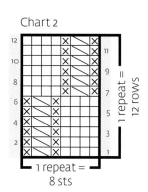

1 repeat = 12 rows

1 repeat = 8 sts

## KNITTING TIP

If you don't like wearing hats, you can just make the brim for a pretty headband. This version is knitted with one strand Alpakka Silke from Sandnes in color 7212 held with one strand Air from Du Store Alpakka in color DL104, on needles U.S. size 6 / 4 mm.

# INGEBORG'S HAT

This Celtic cable pattern is one of my absolutely favorite motifs. It would look particularly nice on a sweater or on the back of a cardigan with the motif repeated many times. Here, I wanted to show how especially pretty it would look as the brim of a hat.

**Sizes** Girl's (Women's)

## Materials
**YARN:** (CYCA #1), Dreamline Sky from Du Store Alpakka, 70% baby alpaca, 30% silk (128 yd/116 m / 25 g), 2 balls color DL306
+ (CYCA #0), Dreamline Soul from Du Store Alpakka, 68% alpaca, 32% nylon (195 yd/177 m / 25 g), 2 balls color DL205
**NEEDLES:** U.S. size 4 / 3.5 mm: short circular and set of 5 dpn + cable needle.
**CROCHET HOOK:** U.S. size D-3 / 3 mm
**GAUGE:** 20 sts in stockinette with the two yarns held together = 4 in / 10 cm.
Adjust needle size to obtain correct gauge if necessary.

**NOTE:** The cabled brim is worked back and forth while the crown is worked in the round.

Holding 1 strand of each yarn together, CO 34 sts. Work back and forth in charted pattern until piece is approx. 20½ (22) in / 52 (56) cm long. BO leaving the last st on needle. Using short circular, pick up and knit 112 (120) sts (including last st of brim) down one long side. Join, pm for beginning of rnd, and purl 1 rnd. Work around in stockinette for 2½ (3¼) in / 6 (8) cm and then purl 1 rnd. Shape top (change to dpn when sts no longer fit around circular):

**Rnd 1:** [K12 (13), k2tog tbl] around.
**Rnd 2:** Knit around.
**Rnd 3:** [K11 (12), k2tog tbl] around.
**Rnd 4:** Knit around.
Rep Rnds 3-4, with 1 less st between decreases each time, until 6 (8) sts rem. Cut yarn and draw end through rem sts; tighten.

## Finishing
Seam the short ends of the cable band. Weave in all ends neatly on WS.

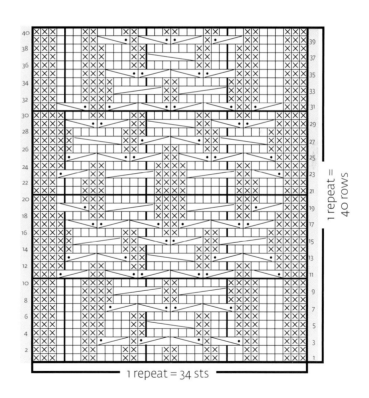

1 repeat = 40 rows

1 repeat = 34 sts

☐   Knit on RS, purl on WS

☒   Purl on RS, knit on WS

C4Fp = Sl 3 sts to cn and hold in front of work, p1, k3 from cn

C4Bp = Sl 1 st to cn and hold in back of work, k3, p1 from cn

C6F = Sl 3 sts to cn and hold in front of work, k3, k3 from cn

C6B = Sl 3 sts to cn and hold in back of work, k3, k3 from cn

# TUNIC WITH HEART CABLES

The tunic is knitted with a single strand of yarn for the body and top of the sleeves, while the long sleeve cuffs, collar, and heart panel are worked with two yarns held together. The body is knitted in the round and then cut open. The cable panel is worked separately and attached before knitting the collar. The yarn is fine, so this tunic is very light and comfortable.

**Sizes** S (M, L, XL)

## Finished Measurements

**CHEST, WITHOUT CABLE PANEL:**
35½ (37, 38½, 40¼) in / 90 (94, 98, 102) cm

**CHEST, WITH CABLE PANEL:** 39½ (41, 42½, 44) in / 100 (104, 108, 112) cm

Length: 29¼ (30, 30¾, 31½) in / 74 (76, 78, 80) cm

**SLEEVE LENGTH, UNDERARM TO CUFF:** 16¼ (16½, 17, 17) in / 41 (42, 43, 43) cm

## Materials

**YARN:** (CYCA #1), Dreamline Air from Du Store Alpakka, 78% Suri alpaca, 22% nylon (257 yd/235 m / 25 g), 2 (2, 2, 2) balls color DL118 + (CYCA #0), Dreamline Soul from Du Store Alpakka, 68% alpaca, 32% nylon (195 yd/177 m / 25 g), 7 (7, 8, 8) balls color DL205

**NEEDLES:** U.S. sizes 6 and 8 / 4 and 5 mm: long and short circulars and set of 5 dpn + cable needle.

**GAUGE:** 30 sts in stockinette with Soul on U.S. size 6 / 4 mm needles = 4 in / 10 cm.
Adjust needle sizes to obtain correct gauge if necessary.

## Body

With Soul and smaller size circular, CO 271 (283, 295, 307) sts; join, being careful not to twist cast-on row. Pm for beg of rnd and at each side = 150 (156, 162, 168) sts for back and 121 (127, 133, 139) sts for front. **NOTE:** Also pm at center st of front—this st will be purled throughout. There are 31 fewer stitches for the front because the heart cable panel will be sewn in afterwards. Work around in stockinette until piece measures 5¼ (6, 6¾, 7½) in / 13 (15, 17, 19) cm. On the next rnd, decrease 4 sts: knit until 2 sts before side marker, CDD (= centered double decrease—sl 2 sts as if to knit tog, k1, p2sso). Work until 2 sts before side marker and decrease with CDD. Decrease the same way every 10th rnd a total of 10 times = 231 (243, 255, 267) sts rem. Continue in stockinette until piece measures 22¾ (23¾, 24½, 25¼) in / 58 (60, 62, 64) cm. BO 6 sts on each side of the markers for the underarms. Set piece aside and make sleeves.

## Sleeves

With larger size dpn and 1 strand each Soul and Air held together, CO 54 (54, 60, 60) sts. Join, pm for beg of rnd (= center of underarm), and work around in pattern following Chart 1. When sleeve is 4¾ (4¾, 5¼, 5¼) in / 12 (12, 13, 13) cm long, increase 1 st on each side of marker every 8th rnd 3 times = 60 (60, 66, 66) sts. Work new sts into pattern. When sleeve measures 9½ (9½, 9¾, 9¾) in / 24 (24, 25, 25) cm, change to smaller needles and work in stockinette only with Soul. *At the same time*, increase 1 st at the center of each cable using M1 (lift strand between 2 sts and knit into back loop) = 70 (70, 77, 77) sts. Continue in stockinette, increasing 1 st at each side of marker on every 8th rnd 7 times = 84 (84, 91, 91) sts. When sleeve measures 16¼ (16½, 17, 17) in / 41 (42, 43, 43) cm, BO 6 sts on each side of marker for underarm. Set sleeve aside and make another the same way.

## Raglan Shaping

Place all the pieces, with body and sleeve underarms matching) on the long, smaller size circular = 347 (359, 387, 399) sts total. Pm between each piece = 4 markers. Shape the raglan on each side of each marker as follows:
Knit until 3 sts rem before marker, ssk, k1, slm, k1, k2tog. Decrease the same way on every other rnd until raglan shaping measures 7½ (7½, 8, 8) in /19 (19, 20, 20) cm. BO 20 sts at center front. Now work back and forth, continuing the raglan shaping as set, and, *at the same time*, shaping on each side of neck: BO 3 sts once, 2 sts 2 times, 1 st 3 times. Set piece aside.

Chart 1

Chart 2

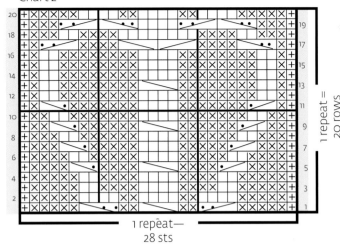

1 repeat =
20 rows

1 repeat—
28 sts

| | |
|---|---|
| ⊞ | Edge st (knit on all rows) |
| ☐ | Knit on RS, purl on WS |
| ⊠ | Purl on RS, knit on WS |
| ⬡ | C3Fp = Sl 2 sts to cn and hold in front of work, p1, k2 sts from cn |
| ⬡ | C3Bp = Sl 1 st to cn and hold in back of work, k2, p1 from cn |
| ⬡ | C4F = Sl 2 sts to cn and hold in front of work, k2, k2 from cn |
| ⬡ | C4B = Sl 2 sts to cn and hold in back of work, k2, k2 from cn |
| ⬡ | C4Fp = Sl 2 knit sts to cn and hold in front of work, p2, k2 from cn |
| ⬡ | C4Bp = Sl 2 purl sts to cn and hold in back of work, k2, p2 from cn |

## Cable Panel

With larger size dpn and one strand each Soul and Air held together, CO 28 sts and purl 1 row. Work the cable panel back and forth, following Chart 2. Work until panel is same length as tunic front = 29¼ (30, 30¾, 31½) in / 74 (76, 78, 80) cm. Place sts on a holder.

## Finishing of Cable Panel

Now it's time to cut the body open up the center front. You can either machine-stitch lines on each side of the central purl st or you use the crocheted "steek" method. There is a good description of steeking on YouTube: https://www.youtube.com/watch?v=OROeKEj57Nk. If you machine-stitch, make 3 lines of fine stitching on each side of the purl stitch so the piece won't unravel. If you steek, you can sew an extra line of back stitching after crocheting on each side to be certain that the work won't unravel. Carefully cut the piece open between the center lines of stitching. Pin the panel to the body and, using Soul, graft the panel to the body through the inner stitch loop of the panel's edge stitches.

## Collar

With larger size dpn and one strand each Soul and air held together, pick up and knit about 130-150 sts around the neckline, including over the panel. Turn the work so the WS is facing out and work a decrease round: (K2tog, k1) around but *not* over the panel. Change to larger size circular and work following Chart 1. When collar measures 2 in / 5 cm, increase 1 st at the beginning of each section of purl sts = 3 purls between each cable. Increase every 2 in / 5 cm, but, the next time you increase, work M1 at the end of the purl st section. Increase on alternating sides of the cables every 2 in / 5 cm until have 6 purl sts between the cables. When collar measures 8 in / 20 cm, BO with knit over knit and purl over purl.

## Finishing

Seam the underarms. With a strand of Soul and crochet hook, work 3 rnds of sc around lower edge of tunic and then work 1 rnd crab st (sc worked from left to right).
Weave in all ends neatly on WS. Gently steam press the lower edge of tunic under a damp pressing cloth.

# WOMEN'S ARAN WRAP SWEATER

This wrap sweater began as a shawl, then became a "soul warmer," and, finally, a sweater. I am very pleased with the result. Several cables in combination = Aran!

**Sizes** S/M (L/XL)

**Finished Measurements**
**Chest:** 37¾ (41) in / 96 (104) cm when slightly stretched
**Total length:** 27¼ (28¾) in / 69 (73) cm

**Total length, including edging:** 31½ (33) in / 80 (84) cm
**Sleeve length:** 18¼ (19) in / 46 (48) cm

**Materials**
**Yarn:** (CYCA #4), Carpe Diem from Lang Yarns, 70% Merino wool, 30% alpaca (98 yd/90 m / 50 g), 17 (19) balls [= 850 (900) g] color 714.0026
**Needles:** U.S. sizes 8 and 10 / 5 and 6 mm: circulars (70 in / 180 cm circular U.S. size 10 / 6 mm for outer band) + cable needle.
**Gauge:** 16 sts in stockinette = 4 in / 10 cm.

Chart 1

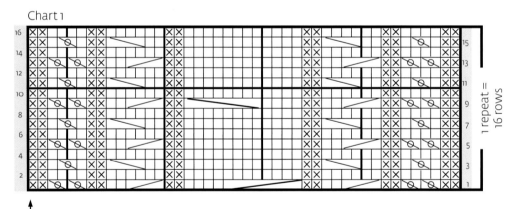

1 repeat = 16 rows

Chart 3

↑
Work 6 sts at the end of the front for size L/XL = purl on RS, knit on WS

Chart 2

| | |
|---|---|
| □ | Knit on RS, purl on WS |
| ☒ | Purl on RS, knit on WS |
| ⟍ | Sl 1 Tw = Sl 1 tbl, yo, k1, pass slipped st over the 2 sts (the yarnover and knit st) |
| ╱ | C4B = Sl 2 sts to cn and hold in back of work, k2, k2 from cn |
| ╲ | C4F = Sl 2 sts to cn and hold in front of work, k2, k2 from cn |
| ╱ | C8B = Sl 4 sts to cn and hold in back of work, k4, k4 from cn |
| ╲ | C8F = Sl 4 sts to cn and hold in front of work, k4, k4 from cn |

Adjust needle size to obtain correct gauge if necessary.

**NOTES:** Read through the entire pattern before you start knitting because there are several places at which you work on various aspects simultaneously. The sweater is worked back and forth except for the ribbed outer band which is worked in the round. Always slip the first stitch of each row = edge st.

### Front and Top of Back
With larger needles, CO 44 (50) sts and purl 1 row on WS. Continue in cable pattern on Chart 1. You should knit 6 extra stitches at the left side for size L/XL. When piece measures 63 (64½) in / 160 (164) cm, BO.

### Lower Part of Back
Fold the front in half and measure out to the center. Pm. Pick up and knit 92 (102) sts = 46 (51) sts on each side of the marker. K1 (edge st), p3 (9), work in pattern following Chart 2, Chart 1, and then Chart 2. End with p3 (9), k1. Continue as set until the back, including the top part, measures 27¼ (28¾) in / 69 (73) cm.

### Sleeves
With larger needles, pick up and knit 72 (78) sts around the armhole and work each sleeve from the top down. Work back and forth in k2, p2 ribbing with the Chart 3 pattern over the center 4 sts. Decrease 1 st at each side on every 6th row until 38 (42) sts rem. When sleeve is 18¼ (19) in / 46 (48)

cm long, BO in ribbing. Seam underarms and side seams. Weave in ends on WS.

### Ribbed Band around Body
With smaller size long circular, pick up and knit stitches all around the outer edge of wrap = approx. 480 (488) sts (make sure that the stitch count is a multiple of 4). Join; pm for beg of rnd and (using a different color/style marker) at each "corner" at the front of each front piece. Work around in k2, p2 ribbing, increasing 1 st on each side of the two center stitches at corner of each front. Increase on every other rnd. When band measures 4¼ in / 11 cm, BO in ribbing.

# MEN'S ARAN SWEATER

The Women's Aran Wrap Sweater of course leads to a men's version with somewhat different cables and a darker beige color. See another photo of it at the front of the book which shows the cables on the back.

**Sizes** XS (S, M, L, XL)

## Finished Measurements
**Chest:** 34¾ (37¾, 40¼, 44, 48) in / 88 (96, 102, 112, 122) cm when slightly stretched
**Total length:** 25¼ (26, 26¾, 27½, 28¼) in / 64 (66, 68, 70, 72) cm
**Sleeve length, underarm to cuff:** 19 (19¼, 19¼, 19¼, 19¾) in / 48 (49, 49, 49, 50) cm

## Materials
**Yarn:** (CYCA #4), Carpe Diem from Lang Yarns, 70% Merino wool, 30% alpaca (98 yd/90 m / 50 g), 13 (13, 14, 15, 16) balls color 714.0339
**Needles:** U.S. sizes 8 and 10 / 5 and 6 mm + cable needle.
**Notions:** leather cord, about 36 in / 90 cm long, and 3 horn buttons
**Gauge:** 20 sts in ribbing, lightly stretched = 4 in / 10 cm. Adjust needle sizes to obtain correct gauge if necessary.

**Note:** The sweater is worked back and forth.

## Shaping Tips For The Left Front
Work in ribbing over the first 13 sts, sl 1, k1, psso (or ssk) and then continue in pattern and ribbing.

## Shaping Tips For Right Front
Work in ribbing over the first 17 (21, 25, 29, 33) sts, continue in charter pattern until 2 sts rem in pattern, k2tog and end with 13 sts ribbing.

## Back
With smaller needles, CO 92 (100, 108, 116, 124) sts and then begin ribbing:
K1, (p2, k2) until 3 sts rem and end with p2, k1. Continue in ribbing until piece measures 2¾ in / 7 cm. Change to larger needles and work in ribbing and charted pattern as follows: Rib as for lower edge over the first 19 (23, 27, 31, 35) sts, work Chart 1 pattern, and then rib over rem 19 (23, 27, 31, 35) sts. Continue in rib and charted pattern as set until piece measures 18½ in / 47 cm.
*Shape armholes:* At each side, BO 3 (3, 3, 3, 3) sts once, 2 sts 1 (1, 1, 2, 2) times, 1 st 4 (2, 3, 3, 4) times. Work without further decreases until piece measures 25¼ (26, 26¾, 27½, 28¼) in / 64 (66, 68, 70, 72) cm. BO.

## Left Front
With smaller needles, CO 48 (52, 56, 60, 64) sts and then begin ribbing:
K1, (k2, p2) until 3 sts rem and end with k3. Continue in ribbing until piece measures 2¾ in / 7 cm. Change to larger needles and work in ribbing and charted pattern as follows: Rib as for lower edge over the first 13 sts, work Chart 1 pattern, and then rib over rem 17 (21, 25, 29, 33) sts. Continue in rib and charted pattern

as set until piece measures 18½ in / 47 cm. Shape armhole as for back and, *at the same time*, shape neck: BO 1 st at neck on every other row a total of 15 (16, 17, 18, 19) times—see Shaping Tips for Left Front. When front is same length as back, place the first 13 sts on a holder and BO rem sts for shoulder.

## Right Front
Work as for left front but mirror-image. Shape neck as described under Shaping Tips for Right Front. When right front is same length as back, place the 13 ribbed sts on a holder and BO rem sts for shoulder.

## Sleeves
With smaller needles, CO 48 (48, 52, 52, 52) sts and then begin ribbing:
K1, (p2, k2) until 3 sts rem and end with p2, k1. Continue in ribbing until piece measures 2¾ in / 7 cm. Change to larger needles and work in ribbing and charted pattern as follows: Rib as for lower edge over the first 19 (19, 21, 21, 21) sts, work Chart 2 pattern, increasing 2 sts at center of sleeve so chart corresponds, and then rib over rem 19 (19, 21, 21, 21) sts. Continue in rib and charted pattern and, *at the same time*, increase 1 st at each side on every 6th row until there are 76 (78, 78, 80, 82) sts. When sleeve measures 19 (19¼, 19¼, 19¼, 19¾)

## Chart 1

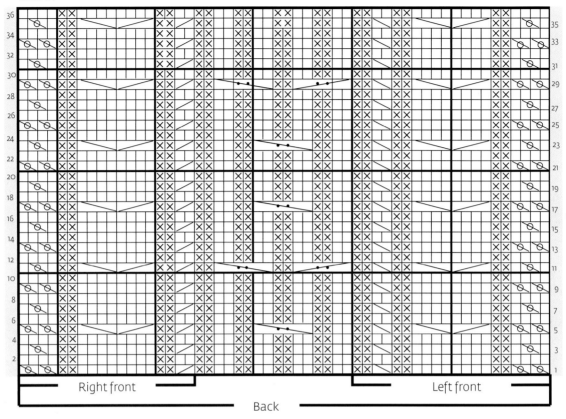

Right front | Back | Left front

---

in / 48 (49, 49, 49, 50) cm, shape sleeve cap: on each side, BO 3 sts 3 times, 2 sts 5 times, 3 sts 1 time. BO rem sts when sleeve measures 22½ (23¼, 23¼, 23¼, 23¾) in / 57 (59, 59, 59, 60) cm.

**Finishing**
Seam the shoulders. Place held sts of left front onto smaller needles and continue the ribbed edge until piece reaches center back; BO. Work the held sts of right front the same way. Seam the short ends of the band as invisibly as possible and then seam band to back neck. Attach sleeves and seam sides.

Cut a 4¾ in / 12 cm length of leather cord and thread through the holes on the horn button. Attach the button to the left front by threading the cord to the

wrong side of the sweater 2¾ in / 7 cm up from the cast-on edge and ⅜ in / 1 cm in from the edge. Knot firmly. Attach the other 2 buttons with the leather cords the same way, spacing them about 8 in / 20 cm apart. Cut three 6 in / 15 cm lengths of the leather cord and attach opposite

buttons as button loops; knot firmly.

## Chart 2

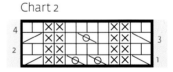

|  | Knit on RS, purl on WS |
|---|---|
| ☒ | Purl on RS, knit on WS |
| ◩ | Sl 1 Tw = Sl 1 tbl, yo, k1, pass slipped st over the 2 sts (the yarnover and knit st) |
| ◸ | C2F = Sl 1 st to cn and hold in front of work, k1, k1 from cn |
| ◹ | C2B = Sl 1 st to cn and hold in back of work, k1, k1 from cn |
| ▱ | C4B = Sl 2 sts to cn and hold in back of work, k2, k2 from cn |
| ▱ | C4F = Sl 2 sts to cn and hold in front of work, k2, k2 from cn |
| ▱ | C6F Rib = Sl 2 knit and 2 purl sts to cn and hold in front of work, k2, sl 2 purl sts to left needle and purl, k2 from cn |
| ▱ | C6B Rib = Sl 2 knit and 2 purl sts to cn and hold in back of work, k2, sl 2 purl sts to left needle and purl, k2 from cn |

# BOLERO

Sometimes it's nice to just have something to sling over your shoulders. I think shawls are pretty on others but I prefer something over my arms and shoulders that won't slide down. Hence this bolero!

**Size** One size

**Total length:** 62¼ in / 158 cm

## Materials
**YARN:** (CYCA #4) Cotinga from Dale Garn, 70% Merino wool, 30% alpaca (87 yd/80 m / 50 g), 9 balls color 2431
**NEEDLES:** U.S. sizes 8 and 10 / 5 and 6 mm + cable needle.
**CROCHET HOOK:** U.S. size H-8 / 5 mm
**GAUGE:** 18 sts on larger needles = 4 in / 10 cm.
Adjust needle sizes to obtain correct gauge if necessary.

With smaller needles, CO 44 sts and work in (k1tbl, p1) ribbing for 4¾ in / 12 cm—but, at 2¾ in / 7 cm and 4 in / 10 cm, CO 1 st at each side. When piece measures 4¾ in / 12 cm, on last row (WS), increase on every 3rd st to 63 sts total. Change to larger needles (don't worry if the yarn ball band says to use U.S. 8 / 5 mm) and work in pattern following the chart. On every 8th row, increase 1 st at each side (purl these sts on RS and knit on WS) until piece measures 21¾ in / 55 cm. Pm at each side. From this point, increase only 1 st at the left side on every 6th row a

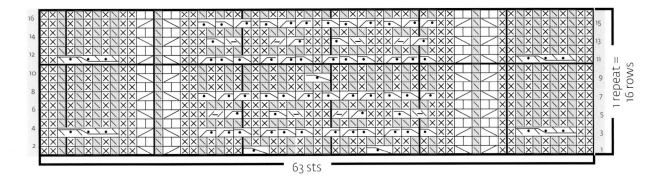

1 repeat = 16 rows

63 sts

total of 5 times. *At the same time,* when the piece is 4¾ in / 12 cm from the marker, shape back neck on the right side as follows: BO 1 st 2 times and 2 sts once. When piece measures 5½ in / 14 cm, from marker, continue without shaping until piece measures 11 in / 28 cm. Now BO 1 st on left side on every 6th row a total of 5 times. *At the same time,* when the opening for the back neck measures 8 in / 20 cm from the last decrease, increase at right side: CO 2 sts once and 1 st 2 times. When piece measures 4¾ in / 12 cm from last decrease for back neck, BO 1 st on each side on every 8th row. Place a new marker at each side. From this point, work in pattern for 17 in / 43 cm. On the last, WS row, k2tog to eliminate every 3rd st = 48 sts rem. Change to smaller needles and work (k1tbl, p1) ribbing, decreasing 1 st at each side at ¾ in / 2 cm and 2 in / 5 cm. BO when ribbing measures 4¾ in / 12 cm.

| | |
|---|---|
| ☒ | Purl on RS, knit on WS |
| ◰ | Twisted knit on RS, twisted purl on WS |
| ⬓ | C2F = Sl 1 st to cn and hold in front of work, k1, k1 from cn |
| ⬔ | C2B = Sl 1 st to cn and hold in back of work, k1, k1 from cn |
| ⬓ | Tw2L = Sl 1 st to cn and hold in front of work, k1tbl, k1tbl from cn |
| ⬔ | Tw2R = Sl 1 st to cn and hold in back of work, k1tbl, k1tbl from cn |
| ⬔ | C2BTw Rib = Sl 1 st to cn and hold in back of work, k1tbl, p1 from cn |
| ⬓ | C2FTw Rib = Sl 1 st to cn and hold in front of work, p1, k1tbl from cn |
| ⬔ | C3FTw Rib = Sl 2 sts to cn and hold in front of work, k1tbl, sl 1 st back on left needle and purl it, k1tbl from cn |
| ⬔⬔ | C7FTw Rib = Sl 3 sts to cn and hold in front of work, (k1tbl, p1, k1tbl, p1), and then k1tbl, p1, k1tbl from cn |

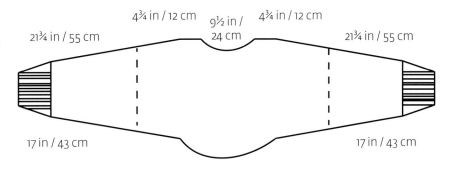

4¾ in / 12 cm    9½ in / 24 cm    4¾ in / 12 cm

21¾ in / 55 cm                                    21¾ in / 55 cm

17 in / 43 cm                                      17 in / 43 cm

## Finishing

Place piece with RS facing RS lengthwise. Measure 17 in / 43 cm from ribbing on right sleeve; pm. Seam the sleeve up to the marker. Do the same on the left side. Turn work.

## Edging

With smaller needles, pick up and knit 268 sts from the center of back neck and around the entire opening. Pm under each sleeve where the seam ends. Work in (k1tbl, p1 tbl) ribbing.

*At the same time,* increase 1 st on each side of the marker for the gusset—increase on every other row a total of 8 times = 16 sts increased under each sleeve. BO with twisted knit and purl sts.

# BAG

Here's a nice, big bag for your handwork or other things. In order to hold its shape, you can, for example, sew in a shopping bag of the type you can buy at a grocery store or make a fabric lining as I did here. I sewed in a lining with a somewhat heavy fabric that I had lying around. Now the bag will keep its shape well.

## Finished Measurements
13½ x 13½ in / 34 x 34 cm

## Materials
**YARN:** (CYCA #5) Easy from Sandnes, 100% wool (55 yd/50 m / 50 g), 9 balls (450 g) color 6052
**NEEDLES:** U.S. sizes 10 and 11 / 6 and 8 mm: circulars + cable needle.
**CROCHET HOOK:** U.S. size J-10 / 6 mm
**NOTIONS:** Two wood handles and fabric or shopping bag for lining

## Front
With larger needles, CO 66 sts and work in pattern following Chart 1. The repeat is worked twice across. Work until piece measures approx. 13½ in / 34 cm and make sure that you finish as shown on the chart. BO with smaller needles to avoid an edge that hangs unevenly.

## Back
Work as for front.

## Side Edges and Base
Work in one piece. With larger needles, CO 18 sts. Work in pattern following Chart 2 until strip measures about 41 in / 104 cm. Do not bind off because you might need to adjust the length.

## Finishing
Place the front and strip with the side edge and base RS facing RS; pin together. If the strip is the right length, BO. If it is too short, work a few more rows. Graft the pieces together through the outermost stitch loops. Place the back and opposite side of the strip RS facing RS and pin together. Graft through the outermost stitch loops.

## Edging around the top
Use the crochet hook to edge the top as follows: work (2 sc, skip 1 st) around. Finish with 1 rnd crab st (sc worked from left to right).

Weave in all ends neatly on WS. Sew a handle centered on the front and another centered on the back. If you prefer, you can instead knit a long strap so you can use the bag as a shoulder bag. Sew in lining.

Chart 1 (front and back)

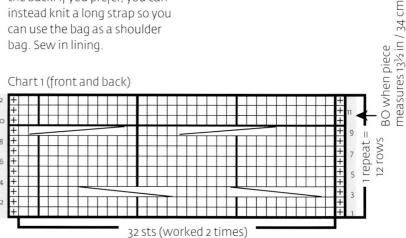

32 sts (worked 2 times)

1 repeat = 12 rows

BO when piece measures 13½ in / 34 cm

## Chart 2 (side edge and base)

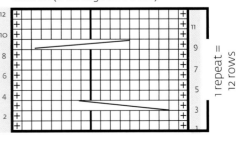

1 repeat = 12 rows

☐  Knit on RS, purl on WS

⊞  Edge st (sl 1 knitwise wyb at beg of row and p1 at end of row)

◢  C10F = Sl 5 sts to cn and hold in front of work, k5, k5 from cn

◢  C10B = Sl 5 sts to cn and hold in back of work, k5, k5 from cn

# CELTIC-INSPIRED SWEATER

I found these pattern combinations in a Japanese pattern book. The designs are made by placing stitches onto a cable needle and wrapping the yarn around the stitches. I think that the different patterns are totally fantastic together. I knitted them back and forth but you can work on a circular in the round. The sweater can be worn by men or women.

**Sizes** S (M, L, XL, XXL, XXXL)

## Finished Measurements
**CHEST:** 38½ (41, 44, 46½, 48¾, 52) in / 98 (104, 112, 118, 124, 132) cm
**TOTAL LENGTH:** 26 (26¾, 27½, 28¼, 29¼, 30) in / 66 (68, 70, 72, 74, 76) cm
**SLEEVE LENGTH:** 19 (19¼, 19¼, 19¼, 20, 20½) in / 48 (49, 49, 49, 50, 52) cm

## Materials
**YARN:** (CYCA #4) Cotinga from Dale Garn, 70% Merino wool, 30% alpaca (87 yd/80 m / 50 g), 15 (16, 17, 18, 19, 20) balls color 0020
**NEEDLES:** U.S. sizes 7 and 8 / 4.5 and 5 mm + cable needle
**GAUGE:** 20 sts in pattern on larger needles = 4 in / 10 cm. Adjust needle sizes to obtain correct gauge if necessary.

**NOTE:** Chart 1 on the next page is so large that you have to turn the book sideways to read the chart properly. You might want to make an enlarged copy instead.

## Back
With smaller needles, CO 98 (104, 112, 118, 124, 132) sts. Work 2¾ in / 7 cm in twisted rib: (K1tbl, p1) on RS and (K1, p1tbl on WS). Change to larger needles and continue in charted pattern, working reverse stockinette (purl on RS, knit on WS) over the first and last 9 (12, 16, 19, 22, 26) sts. Work in pattern as set until piece measures 24¾ (25½, 26½, 27¼, 28, 28¾) in / 63 (65, 67, 69, 71, 73) cm. Place the center 18 (24, 32, 38, 44, 52) sts on a holder and work each side of back neck separately. At neck edge, on every other row, BO 2 sts 2 times, and, *at the same time*, shape shoulder by binding off 12 sts 3 times = no sts rem (fasten off loop of last st bound-off).

## Front
Work as for back, but, when piece measures 24½ (25¼, 26, 26¾, 27½, 28¼) in / 62 (64, 66, 68, 70, 72) cm, place the center 10 (16, 24, 30, 36, 44) sts on a holder and work each side of neck separately. At neck edge, BO 3 sts once, 2 sts once, 1 st 3 times, and, *at the same time*, shape shoulder by binding off 12 sts 3 times = no sts rem (fasten off loop of last st bound-off).

## Sleeves
With smaller needles, CO 42 (42, 44, 46, 46, 48) sts. Work 2¾ in / 7 cm in twisted rib as for lower edge of body, but, on the last WS row, increase 1 st = 43 (43, 45, 47, 47, 49) sts (the increase is so that the pattern comes out evenly). Change to larger needles, and continue in pattern following Chart 2 then Chart 3, and then Chart 2 again. *At the same time*, work the first and last 2 (2, 3, 4, 4, 5) sts in reverse stockinette. Increase 1 st at each side on every 5th row until there are 87 (87, 91, 95, 95, 99) sts. Work the new sts in reverse stockinette. When sleeve is 19 (19¼, 19¼, 19¼, 20, 20½) in / 48 (49, 49, 49, 50, 52) cm long, BO across.

## Finishing
Seam the front and back shoulders. Measure to find the center of the top of the sleeve and pin to shoulder seam on body, with RS facing RS. Attach sleeve with whip st by sewing through the outermost stitch loop on both the body and the sleeve. This makes a smooth seam. Attach opposite sleeve. Seam sides and sleeves with RS facing RS.

## Neckband
Place the 18 (24, 32, 38, 44, 52) held sts onto a short smaller size circular and knit sts; pick up and knit 18 sts (all sizes) along neck, place 10 (16, 24, 30, 36, 44) held sts onto circular, knit sts, and then pick up and knit 18 sts (all sizes), on other side of neck = 64 (76, 92, 104, 116, 132) sts total. Join and work around in (k1tbl, p1) ribbing for 1¼ in / 3 cm. BO loosely.

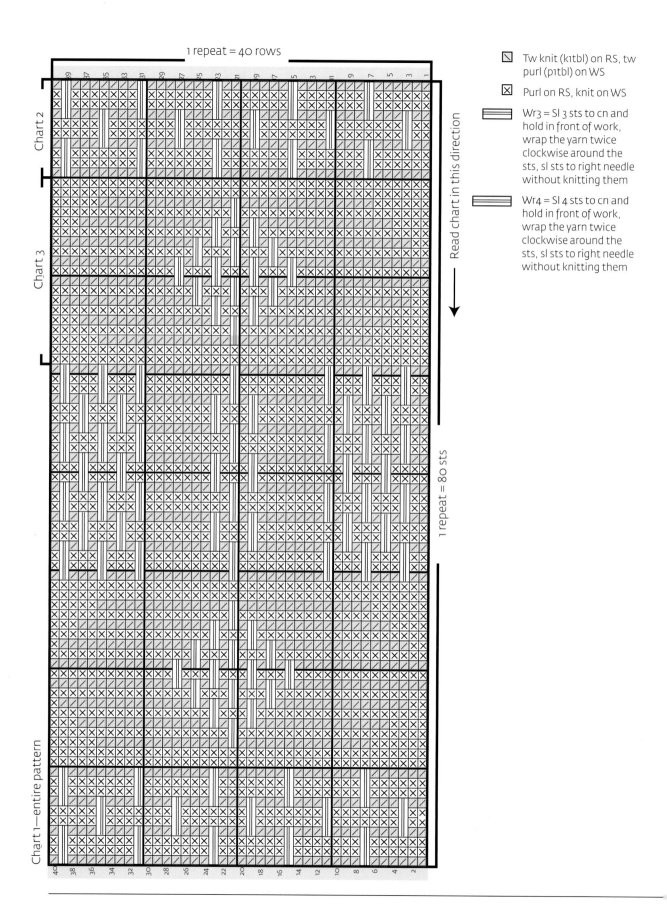

1 repeat = 40 rows

Chart 2

Chart 3

Read chart in this direction

1 repeat = 80 sts

Chart 1—entire pattern

☐ Tw knit (k1tbl) on RS, tw purl (p1tbl) on WS

☒ Purl on RS, knit on WS

Wr3 = Sl 3 sts to cn and hold in front of work, wrap the yarn twice clockwise around the sts, sl sts to right needle without knitting them

Wr4 = Sl 4 sts to cn and hold in front of work, wrap the yarn twice clockwise around the sts, sl sts to right needle without knitting them

# THROW

Have you knitted all the swatches in the book? Join them into a throw. So that the throw would be big enough and the cable blocks would be distinct, I added ten simple stockinette blocks. If you want to make a throw like this one, just spread all the swatches out on the floor and place a few stockinette-knit blocks intermittently—one block for each row. They will be a little wider than the cable blocks, but that's on purpose, since some of the cable patterns draw the knitting in across the width. The stockinette blocks compensate for that loss of width.

## Finished Measurements
39½ in / 100 cm wide and 59 in / 150 cm long

## Materials
**YARN:** (CYCA #3) Lerke from Dale Garn, 52% cotton, 48% Merino wool (125 yd/114 m / 50 g)
**YARN AMOUNTS:**
18 balls color 3041
1 ball color 2425
**NEEDLES:** U.S. size 6 / 4 mm + cable needle
**CROCHET HOOK:** U.S. size E-4 / 3.5 mm

**NOTE:** The throw is composed of 60 blocks—ten lengthwise and six across. Most of the blocks with cable patterns measure 6 x 6 in / 15 x 15 cm. The stockinette blocks have 40 sts and 40 rows.

## Finishing
Lay the blocks on the floor a little randomly or arrange them in the same order you see in the photo on the next page. Since some of the cable blocks are narrower than others, make sure that you have a narrow pattern block in each row together with a wider/stockinette block—then your throw will look like mine. First, sew the six bottom tier blocks together, or, if you prefer, crochet the blocks together. Join the next six blocks and then seam the two strips. Continue seaming until all the blocks are joined to form the entire throw.

## Edging
**Rnd 1:** Work a round of single crochet all around the throw, working 3 sc in each corner st.
**Rnd 2:** Work (ch 5, 1 dc in the 3rd ch, skip 3 sc, 1 sc in next st) around.

# ACKNOWLEDGMENTS

I want to send a huge thank you to all the yarn companies for their generous donations of yarn for the swatches and most of the projects: Sandnes Garn, Dale Garn, and Du Store Alpakka, as well as the yarn shop, Tjorven, for Lang Yarns.

A big thank you for the sporty contributions of my models: Johanne, Sigrid, Ingeborg, Frode, Randi, and Petter.

A thousand thanks to my editor, Toril Blomquist, and photographer Guri Pfeifer, who believed in the project—and not least, to Inger Margrethe Karlsen and Karin Range who said yes!
The very biggest thanks go to Tormod—my dear husband—who so patiently endures times of great frustration, yarn balls, and knitting needles 365 days a year.

## Resources

*Aran Knitting.* Alice Starmore (ISBN-978-0-486-47842-5)
*250 Knitting Patterns Book.* Hitomi Shida (ISBN-4-529—4176-X)
*The Very Easy Guide to Cable Knitting.* Lynne Watterson (ISBN-978-03-1260899-6)
Wikipedia

# YARN INFORMATION

**Webs – America's Yarn Store**
75 Service Center Road
Northampton, MA 01060
800.367.9327
www.yarn.com
customerservice@yarn.com

**SwedishYarn.com**
800.331.5648
www.swedishyarn.com
info@swedishyarn.com

**Mango Moon Yarns**
312 S Elm Street
Owosso, MI 48867
989.723.5259
www.mangomoonyarns.com
info@mangomoonyarns.com

If you are unable to obtain any of the yarn used in this book, it can be replaced with a yarn of a similar weight and composition. Please note, however, the finished projects may vary slightly from those shown, depending on the yarn used. Try www.yarn-sub.com for suggestions.

For more information on selecting or substituting yarn, contact your local yarn shop or an online store; they are familiar with all types of yarns and would be happy to help you. Additionally, the online knitting community at Ravelry.com has forums where you can post questions about specific yarns. Yarns come and go so quickly these days and there are so many beautiful yarns available.